Praise for

You'll Make It (and They Will Too)

"This is the book every parent raising a teenager needs. Amy reminds us—as only she can with her genuine wit, wisdom, and love—that we're not alone in our struggles and that our teens will come back to us. As a longtime fan of Amy's, I turn to her advice time and time again while raising my own teens. I know you will too."

—LESLIE MEANS, founder and owner of
Her View From Home LLC

"Parenting teens doesn't come with a manual, but this book comes as close to one as I've ever read. With refreshing honesty, compassion, and humor, Amy reveals the hard-to-decode core needs of teenagers. Parents experiencing frustration, shame, or hopelessness will find real relief and tangible hope in these pages."

—RACHEL MACY STAFFORD, *New York Times* bestselling
author, speaker, and special-education teacher

"This is the book we parents of teenagers will carry around in purses or stash in the center console of our cars so we can return to it every time we wonder, *Am I going to get through this? Is my kid going to be okay?* With compassion enough to make us feel safe and wisdom enough to help us hold on to hope, Amy Betters-Midtvedt is the mentor and friend we can count on no matter what."

—MIKALA ALBERTSON, MD, family practice doctor and author
of *Everything I Wish I Could Tell You About Midlife*

"Amy shines a spotlight on the importance of putting the relationships we have with our kids ahead of everything else—and that leading with love, acceptance, and grace can help us weather any storm. I found myself nodding as she detailed the complexities of raising kids today, belly laughing at her relatable stories, and choking back tears at the love she pours into her family."

—WHITNEY FLEMING, author of *You're Not a Failure: My Teen Doesn't Like Me Either*

"Amy helps normalize the experience of parenting teens as she talks about the things we desperately need to hear: mental health, faith, social media, friendship, letting go, and more. Her words bring comfort and provide companionship as we come to see that we really aren't the only ones who are trying to make it."

—JEN THOMPSON, creator of Truly Yours

"If you feel like you're stumbling along the path of raising teenagers, Amy Betters-Midtvedt offers a steady hand to hold. She reaches into the dark and deep to shed light, and even humor, where we need it most. This heart-healing, soul-filling, truth-telling book will quickly become a coveted companion that not only helps you survive the teenage years but also invites you to embrace them with confidence and hope."

—MEHR LEE, writer of Raise Her Wild blog

"Amy Betters-Midtvedt has a profound ability to articulate the things we wrestle with as mothers. She makes us feel seen while also offering an extended hand and the hope that we can get through this. This is the perfect tool kit for the harrowing journey that is raising teens."

—JESS JOHNSTON, national bestselling co-author of *I'll Be There (But I'll Be Wearing Sweatpants)*

you'll make it (and they will too)

you'll make it (and they will too)

Everything No One
Talks About When
You're Parenting Teens

Amy Betters-Midtvedt

WATERBROOK

A WaterBrook Trade Paperback Original

Published in the United States by WaterBrook,
an imprint of Random House, a division of
Penguin Random House LLC.

WATERBROOK and colophon are registered trademarks
of Penguin Random House LLC.

Library of Congress Cataloging-in-Publication Data
Names: Betters-Midtvedt, Amy, author.
Title: You'll make it (and they will too) : everything no one talks about when
you're parenting teens / Amy Betters-Midtvedt.
Description: [Colorado Springs] : WaterBrook, [2024] |
Includes bibliographical references.
Identifiers: LCCN 2024000555 | ISBN 9780593601129 (paperback ; alk. paper) |
ISBN 9780593601136 (ebook)
Subjects: LCSH: Parenting—Religious aspects—Christianity. | Parenting.
Classification: LCC BV4529 .B485 2024 | DDC 248.8/45—dc23/eng/20240213
LC record available at https://lccn.loc.gov/2024000555

Printed in the United States of America on acid-free paper

waterbrookmultnomah.com

2 4 6 8 9 7 5 3 1

Book design by Elizabeth A. D. Eno

Most WaterBrook books are available at special quantity
discounts for bulk purchase for premiums, fundraising, and
corporate and educational needs by organizations, churches,
and businesses. Special books or book excerpts also can be
created to fit specific needs. For details, contact
specialmarketscms@penguinrandomhouse.com.

This book is dedicated to the loves of my life:

My dear husband, Todd, without whom this book would not exist in the world for a million reasons.

My children, Ellie, Lily, Thomas, Kate, and Sam, who are my best teachers.

And my parents, Mary and Tom, for all they have taught me about how to parent for relationships and love.

CONTENTS

In the Dark of Night

I was just lying there, body not moving but mind spinning out of control. It was the dark of night, and a million different scenarios presented themselves to my now-wide-awake brain, all of them ominous and highly unlikely. But at two o'clock in the morning, my mind was not reasonable.

I should have known. How had I missed it?

Last week, during a moment when all was (seemingly) calm for the first time in a while after a big batch of teenage trouble, my girl wanted to sleep at a friend's house where she had slept a million times before, and we gave in. We were wary, but she had covered all her bases, promising to call to tell me who was there and then checking in again to tell us about the tents they set up, saying, "It's so much fun, Mom! Thank you for letting me come." We even got a goodnight call from the backyard, and naive me thought, *Maybe things are going to be different. We have clearly turned a corner. Well done, us!*

I actually slept well that night.

The next day I opened Facebook and did not see pictures of her in a backyard tent. No, instead, I was confronted with photo after photo of her dancing on cliffs at some park with her friends. She had been hours away from home, which I could see thanks to her friend's post with pictures of the tomfoolery that outed the lies. A social media win! Let me tell you, rage doesn't begin to describe what I felt scrolling through those images.

But beneath the rage is always the fear, right?

That rage led to a bunch of yelling when she got home, a giant grounding that would last months (she cared not . . . said she would "catch up on her art"), and more sleepless nights for me as I wondered how we had gotten here.

As I think about it, my friend, I have been up at two o'clock in the morning for roughly twenty-two years—the years of nursing babies or trying to make room for myself next to a squirmy toddler or wondering how I was going to do all that needed to be done for the school-age kids. And though we had now reached the years where those kids needed me less during the day, I was awake in the middle of the night more than ever.

Lying awake on any given night, I pictured every single horrible outcome that could happen to my kids: *Lily is heading to the mall tomorrow with friends. I hate that they are going alone. Sam is heading to camp on his first weeklong excursion. What if he can't sleep or they don't supervise him swimming? Kate is about to get her driver's license. What if she is the one to get in an accident on that horrible drive to school? Why do we even let these kids drive? It is madness. And where is Thomas really when his Life360 "accidentally" turns off? And was I right to ground Ellie for two whole months? What on earth am I doing about that kid anyway?*

The not knowing was the worst. There were so many ways the world could hurt them. And so many ways I could get it wrong. My brain raced to find ways to control all the outcomes even though I knew it was impossible.

My thoughts can get so dark in the middle of the night, imagining every disaster. The level of anxiety in my soul sends me walking from room to room to check on my kids. I just need to see them and maybe touch their legs or their foreheads. Each of my children would readily confirm that they have experienced at least one moment of terror opening their eyes to find me bending over them, looking at them, as I tried to find calm and reassure myself that they were okay, at least in that moment.

One night, I had just returned from my wandering and checking and lay staring at the ceiling, listening to my husband breathe through his CPAP machine and struggling not to be jealous of the way that man sleeps. I tried to calm my worried heart. Suddenly a memory came so clearly to my mind that I was transported back in time to when my now-tall kids were still so small.

I could see and smell and feel them—my five babies, all bathed and sweet-smelling and jammied up in little nightgowns and footed pj's, as they ran around the family room, hid behind the curtains, and then threw themselves across the room, crawling all over me and one another. I sat on the couch exhausted in my soul, wishing for bedtime but also in awe that I got to parent these kids. When I couldn't take it another minute, I gathered them in front of me for what our family called the popcorn game.

The popcorn game was one of our favorites. I had made it up one day in a desperate attempt to contain all my crazy offspring in one place. I would sit on the couch, and they would lie on the floor in front of me and pretend they were kernels of popcorn that I would pretend to pop on the stove.

As always, the oldest, Ellie, took control of the group. "Get into position, guys!"

They would all scramble to the floor, Lily helping Sam become a still, little popcorn seed, a position he could maintain for about thirty seconds before wiggling around. Soon all five were curled into little balls, waiting.

My job was to tell them when to pop.

I would pause for a moment to drink in the stillness before saying, "Oh man, I would love some popcorn. Look at these seeds here just lying in the pan. Here I go, turning on the heat. Oh, they are moving all over!"

The kids would start to roll around on the floor, giggling.

"It's getting hotter. Any minute now they will start popping!"

The kid who couldn't wait for another second would jump up and pretend to burst out of their shell.

"Oh my goodness, popcorn is flying everywhere!"

At this, all five kids would jump up and around, bumping into one another and yelling, "Pop! Pop! Pop!"

When the popping got almost out of control, I would say, "All done! I can't wait to dig in!" And all the kids would fall to the floor, still as can be, ready for me to jump in among them and start tickling and pretending to eat them up.

It had provided endless hours of fun over the years and may also show that my kids had a low bar for what qualified as entertainment.

Those days were so sweet and now so very far away. We hadn't played the popcorn game in years. Who knew if they even remembered it.

I had the realization that this game was a moment when I could control their every move. And now as they were becoming teenagers, I felt I had zero control over *any* of their movements, thoughts, or actions, and the odds of them all gathering at my feet because they just wanted to be near me were slim to none unless I was handing out cash or something.

As I looked back during the dark of night, I couldn't help but long for the days when my worries were about smaller things. The little worries are still here, but now there are big worries too—the kind that make you lie awake and wonder where you have gone wrong. Worries like *How do I let them leave and drive actual cars?* and *Why are they handing in zero homework?* feel small when you look at bigger worries like *What if I find alcohol or pot or condoms or a vape pen or something else shocking in their childhood bedroom where their stuffies still live?*

If you are like me, your heart might break a little when these bigger worries actually come true. You might feel betrayed or terrified or let down. And you might feel like it is all your fault.

But it isn't.

These kids are struggling. Our now-tall babies are trying to find their place. They might be slightly terrified or betrayed by their own bodies or minds, and they might even feel *we* have let them down. These kids might feel like every mistake is all their fault (even as they tell you everything is your fault, but don't be fooled).

It isn't.

It's all part of the struggle. You and your kids have to walk some of this journey apart, but you are still in it together.

When our kids are wandering *way* off the path (or onto literal cliffs!), it can feel like nothing is going to be right again. The first time a kid went flat-out off the rails, it threw my heart for a loop. I had tried to use my words to control the situation with my daughter. "Do this! Stop doing that! Listen to me!" None of it worked. Instead, it all got worse—the arriving home late, hiding things under her bed, and telling small lies that seemed like nothing but that actually revealed all the ways she had closed off her heart from us. And with that closed heart she walked forward into bigger and worse things.

I had so much *fear* in my heart for this child. I could see all the mistakes she was making, and I wanted to stand in the way of every single one. And, yes, this probably made all those mistakes look even more tempting, just like when she was little and we put something breakable high out of reach and suddenly that was the thing she *had* to have.

I was terrified of the path she was tromping with wild abandon. Also, this kid was having so much fun on this trail that there didn't seem to be a reason for her to listen to our calls home. Home was boring! What her friends were offering her was way, waaaaay more fun, and they were the ones she was following.

I wanted absolute authority over this kid. I wanted her to *listen to me*! But this was not mine to have. She belongs to God and to herself. Sadly she wasn't listening to God at this time, either, and her self was leading her in the wrong direction. My fear made me want to control her moves, stop time, and keep her home.

I let that trembly, heart-stopping fear call the shots for a while, and it made me reach for all the control.

My love for my dear girl hid behind fear, panic, and a lot of long, long lectures.

Trying to control and punish my way into her heart wasn't working, so I changed direction. I know that on occasion love looks like hard consequences, but mine were coming from fear. And I started to realize that love sometimes looks like letting small things slide. Sometimes it looks like working to get the door open so they will talk to you. Sometimes it looks like giving them space. And it *always* looks like finding all the good in these people. We must remind ourselves they are doing their best; they are good and worthy and just messing up like humans do.

When our kids are actively running off the path away from us, it is a nightmare for us, but they think there is a payoff for them. My oldest now tells us she would weigh being grounded against whatever fun she was about to embark on . . . and decide that fun was completely worth the punishment.

To be honest, not only was I living in fear for her safety, but I also feared what everyone else thought. I remember feeling shame for not being able to *make* my daughter do what she was supposed to be doing. That was what a good mom did, right? A successful mom got her kid to do all the right things in life—have good grades, a pleasant demeanor, and a job they could handle along with all the AP classes and activities that she could watch them participate in and post pictures of on Facebook. Being a good mom meant your kid looked shiny, perfect, and mistake-free. People would stop you in the street and tell you how great your kid was. *That* was success.

So we pretend, don't we? We shine it up for one another and for our kids. Yet pretending is like a wall that rises between you and your child, and big bold letters on their side of the wall spell out, "How this looks is more important than how you feel." But that message will make them run away from that wall and from you.

Because being shiny doesn't cut it. Instead, being a good mom might mean letting a kid break into a million pieces and then helping them put those pieces back together in a way that is somehow both battered and more beautiful. It is doing the work no one ever sees—the work that keeps you in a relationship with your kids in a way that helps them become themselves.

If you want to be included in their growth, you have to let them grow without insisting it looks perfect every step of the way. Love is the tool you will use to do this. It's the only way. Looking at them through the same eyes you used to take in their newborn faces will make it much easier.

We had to let go of this daughter . . . with love. We didn't give up, but we gave her space to make her own mistakes and to own the consequences. We talked it out and worked it out, and sometimes we messed up and tried again. But we kept on coming back to the love and to the relationship, remembering that this kid was doing the best she could and so were we.

So that child who was grounded and who made about a million of my hairs gray? By the one-year anniversary of the Great Grounding, we were walking together again. And as a silly token of goodwill for this new and different path we were on together, we presented her with a necklace that held a small amount of soil from the park where she had been dancing on those cliffs. It was a symbol of all that had changed between us.

We had made it through, and we could laugh about it (now). We had become different, closer. The controlling, terrified me who sat at the table waiting for her to arrive home could never have predicted it, but here we were. The mistakes she made no longer defined her. Instead, the love we had for her won the day, and we sat together as flawed humans doing the best that we could. We were all learning together.

There is so much hope and joy to be found. I have parented and am still parenting my own five kids, ages twelve to twenty-two. None of it is easy. It is messy and filled with so many emotions that make us doubt both ourselves and our kids. In some moments, we are ready to push them out into the world, and in others, we want to hold on to their legs and beg them to stay forever.

So often, all I needed to get through the tough times was to know I was not alone. I am here to tell you that you are not alone either. We will travel together through this book to help you see the beauty where you can and make it through the hard times. Because the hard times will inevitably come, and in those moments we need all the tips, lessons, and *I have been there*s that we can get.

Along my path, I have studied child and adolescent development, leadership, engagement, behavior, and all the things. Because I have been an educator for twenty-five years, I have been around and connected to children for so long that I want to pass all I have learned on to you too.

This book is born from a journey of loving so much that it made me afraid. And in my fear, I spoke not love but authority into the ears of my children way too often, believing it would keep them on the safe, straight, and shiny path I wanted them to take. I didn't realize that every time I tried to control everything, it would make them want to veer not only off the path but also far from my love.

It was a journey of too much talking to my kids about what I thought and not nearly enough listening. Too much worry and not enough letting go.

It was a journey that pulled me away both from what the world was saying and from what I thought a good parent would do. It brought me back directly into my love for my children and to my desire from the very beginning to connect with them deeply in a way that would lead us into a lifetime relationship. It led me to look away from the glory of a passing moment that might impress other humans.

But more than all that, it has been a journey of how my kids and I found our way back to one another—and how you and your family can too.

Because the journey is also about encountering joy and redemption and finding all the wonderful moments with these people who once depended on you for everything. It's about discovering the beauty in their becoming, and celebrating all that they are, just as God made them. It is about helping them find God even though they are asking the hard questions that we start asking too. It is also about the funny and fun parts of parenting our teenagers—because they are flat-out hilarious a lot of the time. I promise you will laugh a little as you tag along through our adventures.

And it really is about the love. I know you have so much of that in your heart for your people.

There is no magic formula for raising teens. (Oh, how I wish there were!) This book is a conversation steeped in stories, hope, and prayer—one in which you may see your own hopes and struggles in the raw and real moments of our parenting journeys shared. And my prayer is that when you feel alone, you can turn to these words and remember you are not—not even a little bit. In each chapter, you will find tips for what you can't do and what you can do, stories of what happened for us, and some really good news about parenting teens. For those moments when you need advice in a hurry, I have included some fast tips (making my long stories short) and a prayer for you to pray when this all just brings you to your knees.

Let's walk together out of the dark of night, through those beginning tween years, and into the struggles around things from curfews to fashion choices. Let's dig into teens dating and what it is like when their friend groups fall apart. Let's not shy away from the hard mental health moments and the launching of our kids, ready or not. Let's talk about the hard pieces, but let's also look at all the joy. Let's celebrate letting our kids become exactly who God created them to be. And together we can walk through this time of continually choosing love and relationship over being right and being obeyed, until we feel like home for our people. All you need to do is bring your love for your kids and turn to the pages that follow.

I hope this book helps you see how to connect with your teenagers in a new way that brings you closer to a real, loving relationship that will last your whole lifetime.

Before I send you into the first chapter, I have a confession. Over and over you will read the word *I* in this book when I really mean *we*. My husband is the other half of that *we*, and he is the man behind this whole operation. I used all those I's to remind you I'm including my perspective but never to imply I was doing this alone. My husband is now and always has been an amazing co-pilot every step of the way, evening me out and calming me down.

It is one thing to figure out how to parent, but it's another to agree about how to do that with another human who was raised differently than you. We have worked hard at it. So please know that when you read the stories of things we have gone through with our kids, if he wasn't there in the story it-self, he was behind the scenes getting a crazed text from me while he worked, putting his arms around me and bolstering me when he arrived home at night, or heading to the kid(s) and putting his arms around them. This man is a one-in-a-million gem, and I am grateful and lucky in this department.

A couple of final notes. Some names have been changed, and in other instances identifying details have been altered a bit to keep a little mystery about the teens involved. Sometimes I have used their actual names, and other times I have left names out of the conversation for the good of the people. All feelings in this book are mine, are true, and were sometimes hard to write, but my teens' feelings and thoughts are theirs to tell. If a teen's story is included in this book, it is with their permission and blessing.

Finally, I'm going to talk to you about struggles our kids go through and about the struggles we might have as parents. We will talk through stories and strategies and thoughts around them, but nothing in this book should ever be a substitute for professional medical advice, diagnosis, treatment, or pre-scribed medication. If you have worries, questions, or doubts regarding your child's well-being or your own, please seek medical and/or psychological treatment from a qualified pro-fessional. This is what I do regularly and there is no substitute for it. Okay, we're done now. Let's get started!

you'll make it (and they will too)

CHAPTER 1

The Tricky Tween to Teen Years

You Are Suddenly Uncool (and Their Brains Are Doing Really Hard Things)

My kids are liars. Every one of my children made me the same promise, and every one of them broke that promise. I have video proof of their lies. I forgive them because they believed their lies when they said them. They couldn't know what was coming, the change that was waiting for them even as they denied my predictions could ever come true.

It went something like this: As a mom of five, I saw the signs repeated each and every time one of the troops turned twelve or thirteen, and I knew just what those signs meant. Like the afternoon when sweet little Lily got dropped off by the bus. She had always been my hugger; her nickname "Lily bug" came from so many days spent calling her our snuggle bug as she tried to be as close to us as possible.

As always, I was ready and waiting to hear about her day and get that hug. But as she stepped onto the curb, I knew something was brewing.

A pang in my heart. This was it. A child who hurried up the walk, not running into my arms so happy to be there. She had *always* run into my arms. Instead, she huffed past me, throwing down her backpack, heading straight up to her room. And as she made her way up the stairs, I still tried to get her to come to me because I had not yet learned some things. "How was your day, kiddo? Want a snack?"

"UGH! No, Mom. I'm not even hungry! Geez!" she said while closing the door.

Apparently seeing me at the end of the day was not the thing that comforted her soul anymore. *Got it.*

The next phases were predictable. Like the sister before her, she started with the eye-rolling. Oh, the eye-rolling. And a little bit of back talk that surprised both of us, frankly. And inevitably there was the moment the hormones surged and she lost her cool when asked whether she had done her homework or could put away the dishes or some such nonsense.

"Mom, stop it. I KNOW! I need to be alone!" she said with a door slam after she headed back to her room following dinner instead of to the couch to watch shows with the family.

As each sibling entered this phase, the littles would look up and one would proclaim with all the love and fierceness in his heart, "Mommy, don't worry. I will *never* act like that. I will always be nice to you and love you."

Liars, one and all.

By the time we got to the third kid stomping from the room, I pulled out my phone and made the last two littles promise me *on video* that they would love me and be sweet to me forever. And I saved that video, even though I flat-out knew these were lies. I also knew I had to let them believe it for now because they couldn't fathom a day when their sweet selves wouldn't want to sit right next to me on the couch.

I, of course, knew the truth. But I really didn't mind living with the lie for a little while longer.

Actually, I preferred it.

What We Can't Do

We cannot stop change, and we cannot hold on too tightly. Throughout my life, I've hated change. Even though change often brought all the big and beautiful gifts, I still resisted it with every inch of my being. I wanted to hold on to whatever was good and keep it forever. I'm a holder-on-er.

In my earlier years, I settled into whatever circumstances life brought my way and dug in hard. I liked how things were, thank you very much. And when my firstborn turned twelve, I got a big dose of change. I had spent twelve years rocking it as a parent. I was great at reading bedtime stories, making lunches, having Friday night movie and dance parties, squeezing onto the couch with all five of my kids, and being able to fix a hurt with a single Band-Aid. I loved every single minute of it.

So, when the tweenage and teenage stuff started happening in my house, I asked myself, *How do I keep this from happening?* Ha! I learned both my soul and heart were pretty much doomed. I couldn't prevent change, as it was inevitable for both my kids and me. Without further warning, I was given a ticket and pushed onto the parenting-a-teenager roller coaster without my consent. I had no choice; I had to figure it out.

The roller coaster goes like this: One minute you feel like you know every single thing about your kid. Heck, she might have even called you her very best friend. She wanted to dress like you and be by you. For an entire decade this child was all yours. Then it all starts to change.

So much weirdness comes when they go back and forth between staying their old selves and becoming their new ones. Conflict will suddenly flow out of nowhere over nothing, and your once-snuggly child will find you super annoying and want nothing to do with you. Then, after you are good and exasperated, she will come out of her room and want to snuggle next to you on the couch like nothing happened at all. One minute she is putting on makeup, trying all sorts of lipsticks and eye shadows she bought with her birthday money, and the next she is in her room with all her American Girl dolls out. Your heart might leap a little. Next, you will overhear your son talking with his friends about which girls are cute, but at bedtime, he will change into his giant Minecraft jammies and ask to be tucked in. You might even spot his lovey hiding out under his pillow. It is just a confusing time for everyone.

Becoming yourself is hard—it might even make a person act a little crazy.

So how are you supposed to treat them at any given moment?

No idea.

Because here is the thing: They don't know either. You are walking a prepubescent land mine of emotions. At any moment you can step into a spot that causes so many tears to flow, and then the next moment everyone is fine. You need to make your peace with the unexpected. There is no other way, and one of you must stay on solid ground—and it won't be them.

It can be shocking to come out of that golden era when our ten- and eleven-year-old children were leading us down the primrose path. This is because we lulled ourselves into believing we had all the parenting nonsense figured out. We had successfully survived raising infants, toddlers, preschoolers, and elementary-school kids, and now we had arrived. *Go, us.*

But these ages were just the wonderful ones where our kids

gained all sorts of independence and still found us charming and delightful. Oh, that glorious time filled with kids who made their own breakfasts and yours too. We got to see the fruits of our labor in these delights who complimented our fashion choices and talked our ears off with awesome stories we understood. Go ahead and have all the nostalgia for ages ten and eleven, and briefly pat yourself on the back for a job well done.

Then gather yourself, my friend, because the truth is . . . we were fools.

We knew nothing.

We were being given a small reprieve before the real stuff hit the fan. The hormones start surging, the bodies start changing, and it is all over but the crying—both theirs and yours.

This brings me to what is happening with them physically. We can see the visible parts of this tweenage phase take place before our eyes as their bodies start changing. It is a really big deal, and you will be super happy if you have been open and honest about all things body when this time hits. The little-kid part of your child will keep you posted about armpit hair for a while, and then the teenage part will go dead silent and run to another aisle when you offer them a deodorant while shopping at Target. You will have to start reading the room to know whether it is an okay time to talk to them about what we refer to around here as the pubening.

And it is not only their outward bodies that are changing. You will notice their behavior is, shall we say, *a little off.* Their brains are going through a huge and rapid phase of development. And this is the reason we see so many confusing things—the wild swings back and forth in their moods; the need to totally separate from us and then cling to us like barnacles for an hour, only to act like we are worm sweat thirty minutes later; the seeming need to push all our buttons or to ask for our ideas and then act like every one of them is the dumbest thing they have ever heard in the history of planet Earth.

Although this phase of rapid development doesn't end until they are roughly twenty-four (*I know!*), this beginning part will sometimes feel excruciatingly long. Our kids will stabilize a bit after the age of fourteen in the emotion department, so hang on to that little fact, my friend.[1] Both their bodies and brains are doing so much, so there is a really good reason these moods are happening.

We cannot ignore the changes and must parent toward them instead of getting locked in a war of wills. The brain changes that enable our kids to separate, go out on their own, have the courage to take risks to try new things, meet new people, become themselves, and develop into independent adults are a good and important thing. It is our job to help them out with some guardrails when their behavior is off the rails, like when they are caught sneaking their phones to check their Snapchat quick even though they are grounded or when they are old enough to drive and get their *third* speeding ticket.

What We Can Do

We can empower our kids and ourselves by reminding us all that these things are normal, and then we can remind ourselves we already have the parenting tricks we need. Some of their behavior is biological, so there is a limit to what we can parent our kids into and out of. We cannot nurture them right out of their nature. Rather, we can nurture them *into* it—for example, by helping them know more about what is happening to them and why. Their biology isn't an excuse to break the rules and act like crazy people, but it is the reason they sometimes do. And we need to remember that the goal isn't to raise kids who never make a mistake but to raise kids who can come to us for understanding and advice when they inevitably do make mistakes.

You might hear them say things like "It seemed like a good idea at the time" after engaging in some sort of foolish behavior. I remember one of my kids walking home late at night instead of calling for a ride like they were supposed to. Of course, when they didn't show up at home and couldn't be found anywhere, there was an all-out search. When we finally found them, all they said was that their phone was dead, so they just walked, which seemed like a good idea to them. *For the actual love, kid, why did you not use the phone that was right there in the building?* They don't always think of the next best thing, just the next weird idea that makes sense to them. It is exhausting.

You might catch your former rule-following tween with his bike helmet on his handlebars instead of on his head because he "forgot" to put it on. If you wonder whether said child is lying to you, yes, he is—but it is because he is too embarrassed to wear a helmet when the other kids aren't, not because he is a liar. Tweens lie because their developing brains keep them doing things that are new, interesting, and in line with their peers much of the time. This is *normal*. Before I understood how their brains work, I really thought that each situation was a tragedy, things were off the rails, and it was all a disaster. Not so. It's normal. Repeat on a loop.

While you remind yourself their changing self is normal, you will also have to remind them. The conversation we dread most is, of course, the one about their bodies that most parents simply whisper about, calling it "the talk." I highly recommend you have said talk with your kids before they hit the tweenage years. Things get so awkward around this time that if you have to bring up s-e-x with them out of nowhere, it might not go well. But if you have laid the groundwork here, you can just keep the door open and not have to introduce them to all the things that are happening to them in real time.

For the record, when I had "the talk" with one of my kids, her response was that this information "ruined her life" and she then burst into tears. So I get it. It is not my favorite parenting day, but it has to be done. You also want to be the one giving them the information. They have heard things on the bus . . . and let me tell you, you do not want them walking around believing the nonsense Marsha told them in hushed tones in the back seat. Trust me. Talk about it early and often, because once the pubening hits, they are embarrassed by everything and this topic most of all. If you have waited, just make your peace with more embarrassment and move forward. You can do it.

It is just as important to talk to them about their brains as about their bodies. Reassure them they are normal, and let them know a little bit of what they might be in for. Let them know all the amazing changes that are happening, and acknowledge that they might feel out of control in their emotions and that you understand it might be hard for everyone sometimes. Let them know it was hard for you. Help them make sense of their own behavior when you can.

Have these big talks when you aren't in the heat of the moment. Pick a time when they are open to listening to you, maybe when you are sitting in the car or on the couch. You will want to tell them things like this:

> During the next few years, you might have times when your emotions are out of control or you really feel like you can't stand me. You will want to be with your friends more than you want to be with us. I want you to know that is normal, and we will understand when that happens.

Your brain is growing and changing right along with your body. Your brain might also want to do all sorts of risky things, which means we might have to make rules that keep you safe but that you might not like. It is also a time when your brain is super creative and is awesome at problem solving—it is even way better at this than our adult brains! How awesome is that? We will try to learn from you.

It is a great time for you to try new things to see if you like them, so think about what kinds of things you might like to try on to see if they are a good fit. All this needs to happen so you will be ready to leave our house someday and be all on your own. Leaving here will sound amazing to you sometimes and really scary other times. It is all normal. And we are here for you and promise not to take it personally when you want to be away from us.

Yes, this means you actually cannot take things personally, so even when you are a flat-out embarrassment in their eyes, repeat to yourself, *They are trying to separate. They need to be independent. It is all a part of growing up.* You don't have to be the brunt of mean behavior, but you can agree to drop them off a few blocks away from school so they won't be seen with you if that's important to them.

Remind yourself this is normal even when you—yes, wonderful, hilarious, loving you—are suddenly a huge embarrassment. Even when they think that you know exactly nothing and that you are an imbecile. Don't even try to tell them about your college degree or about how you run a company or are writing a book. They do not care. You do not understand cool memes, and your taste in shoes is abysmal.

Just go with God and let them bask in their absolutely fake

wisdom when this is where their brains are. It is a phase, but it is a long one, so buckle on up. You are still wonderful, and the rest of the world still thinks you rock. It is them and not you—look in the mirror and repeat this to yourself at least ten times if you start to feel like you are losing it. And remind them continually that they need to use their nice words with everyone, including you, so disrespect isn't going to fly.

This is also a time when you might start to feel triggered or angry or have your own big feelings about all of it. This may be a sign that it actually *is* you and that you have to get your own stuff together because you owe it to your kids to be the best version of you. Hunker down, talk it out, head to therapy, and just do what needs to be done. They need you to show up for them, full stop.

While your kids think you don't know a thing, you do have some tricks up your sleeve. Tweens and toddlers are incredibly similar, as it turns out. Most of what was true for our kids when they were two is true again now. Remember when they would sob if they didn't get the princess cup and they wanted to spend every day dressed like Spider-Man? You thought those days were behind you, didn't you?

You, dear one, were incorrect.

Now the tall kid will inexplicably sob when a sibling grabs the water bottle they wanted to take to school. This kid will also wear only Nike brand white socks and the same two hoodies in rotation. You will feel like you are parenting a giant version of their two-year-old self. But the good news is that some of the same strategies you used on that two-year-old still work. So we can lean back in and pull out our old tricks.

It is time to rely heavily on the same trifecta that worked when they were little: *snacks* (you can actually hand out the same fruit snacks and Goldfish crackers they have always liked, but you now get bonus points for fancy coffees), *showers* (like when they were small and you'd put them in a bath, only now a fancy spa bath might be just the thing—or they can sweat it out in a nice long shower), and *sleep*. Of the three, sleep is king. As their bodies start to grow at a crazy rapid rate, they are often tired and don't even know it. Remember that overtired two-year-old running around at the end of their rope? Back then, often the only thing to do was to put that child in a crib with their lovey and let them snooze it out. Same here. They might not love the suggestion (remember how the two-year-old would kick and struggle and insist they were *not tired*?), but send them to their rooms and give them a nice fuzzy blanket and tiptoe away. Everyone is much happier after a rest.

You need one too, since all this navigating and letting go take a toll on your heart—not only because so many changes are happening but also because you will suddenly see the future coming at you like it is going to hit with warp speed.

The season when you were their whole world is ending, and you may be struggling mightily. It's not an easy place to be. Give yourself all the grace.

What Happened for Us

We have made it through four of our five kids' pubening. Currently my fifth pancake is just entering this stage, and the biggest sign is that I am now wrong about almost everything. (Yes, I called my kid a pancake. I'll explain why in chapter 4.) Every comment I make is met with a "No, Mom, it's actually . . ." It is just a delight, I tell you. I can laugh about it this time around and even tell him, "Welp, looks like your brain is getting ready to move on and do its own thing." About 71 percent of the time he finds this funny and hugs me. The rest of the time? Well, of course he says, "No, Mom, it's actually . . ." and I wonder if I will make it.

I can laugh, but I also need a few tender moments alone in the quiet so I can feel all my feelings about the bittersweetness of it all. I know what is coming, so I need time to pray all the necessary prayers. This time in the quiet has been so important in helping me learn to become a new version of myself as a parent. Because as they change, we must change too.

I've learned that the process of letting go and moving forward doesn't happen all at once. It happens in little moments over many days, and sometimes it feels like grief over a child who isn't even at this stage yet but you can see it coming. Other times it feels like excitement over all the amazingness that child is going to bring to the world. Sometimes, just like when they were two, you cannot wait for a phase to end, but mostly you are now trying to slow down time. And you never really get used to it. You learn to act like you do or have long stretches where this all starts to feel almost normal.

That's all good.

I've heard it many times: We need to toughen up or be happier about them leaving and learn to let go. But I am here to say it's okay if you have a lot of feelings about your kids hitting these first parts of the teenage years and your heart is hurting a little or you feel like crying. Feel those feelings, friend.

On the flip side, if you are cool with it and excited, that is awesome too. Every parent will feel differently when their kids start to act teenager-y. And all your emotions are absolutely okay. You are allowed to feel them and express them. You might not be able to talk about your kids' secrets, but you can talk about how hard all of this is on your heart.

And you *can* complain about being tired. I don't care what anyone says. Even though you are not up with a newborn, you are the kind of tired that warrants complaining. You are *heart* tired, and that is its own thing.

I found if you can let out some of your feelings and deal with what you are going through, you will have a much easier time being a present human who can parent through the exhaustion and sometimes heartache. We need to be able to look into the eyes of our unsure-of-themselves-yet-somehow-annoyed-with-us teenagers and let them know they are okay. It's all part of becoming a grown person, and we love them just as much or even more than the day they arrived in our arms. They need to know we are not mourning and longing all the time for little them. They need to know we love with our whole hearts this slightly taller, more confused, and a little more stinky version of who they are.

The Good News

At this point in my journey, I can tell you a few good things. My launched kids tell me that being open, listening, and loving them no matter what, exactly as they were during those tween years, were the most impactful, positive things I did as a parent. They also point out that when I was too "bossy" or tried to tell them all the time how to do it better, it was hurtful and did not make them change their behavior; instead, it sent them farther away from our guidance. And they admit that even when they said they wanted us farther away, they really loved to be able to crawl back in our laps when needed, even if they didn't totally fit.

I have learned so much from these people I am parenting. And there is beauty in that learning and lots of gifts in the change. Joy comes after and sometimes right in the crazy parts of this age, and you feel so much love for these people all the time. Even when you find yourself not liking them all that much, you still love them with all your heart. I have found such a holy space with my tall, wonderful, exasperating, lovely people. And I want that for you too. I want you to know you are not alone on this ride.

And if you are reading this and your kids are already deep

into the teenage years, know it is okay if you wish things had gone differently. We all have those feelings, and there are times we make missteps. It is inevitable. I am here looking you in the eye and telling you it is never too late to make a change in your parenting. And it is never too late to apologize. I do this a lot around here, and man, I get it.

We are in it together. You will make it. And they will too.

Long Story Short

- Biological changes are happening inside and out for your kids. Knowing and talking about these are good.

- Our kids might swing wildly between acting like children and acting like teenagers. This is frustrating and weird and completely normal.

- Think about how you parented when they were two, and do the things that helped them then. (Don't forget: bed, bath, and snacks.)

- It is okay for you to feel your feelings, whatever they are, and it is okay for them to feel their feelings too. Even the not-so-fun ones.

Dear Lord,

Help me realize that all this letting go is a part of Your divine plan, even the way our sweet, little, good-smelling babies start to pull away and also smell not so good. Please guide my heart during this time to see all the wonderful newness unfolding in this child. Also, help my heart grieve the parts I feel I am losing, because losing that unfettered love of my babies is much harder than I thought it would be.

Help me know the words to say to reassure this child that they are just as You made them and that all the changes that are starting to happen to them are a part of the miracle of Your creation. Help me keep my tongue quiet around them when I want to tell them how cute they used to be and instead tell them how awesome they are now.

And please, dear God, let me help them know that putting on deodorant is now a must and that they absolutely have to shower more because the miracle of Your creation needs washing more frequently. Help me to help them.

Amen.

CHAPTER 2

Getting to Know the New Parts of Your Teenager

Tattoos in the Walmart Parking Lot and Wanting to Ground Them Forever

I spotted the black little star on her wrist and thought it was a drawing made with marker. For whatever reason, kids in my house and kids in my classrooms loved to draw pictures on their body parts and on their friends. When I explained they should really be drawing these pictures on pairs of white Keds (à la 1985), my people looked at me like I was nuts. But honestly, our moms didn't realize they were blessed that we messed up our shoes rather than our actual selves.

This particular drawing on my child seemed to be lasting quite a long time. After many days spent at the lake without this little star washing off from her wrist, I felt a knot in the pit of my stomach. How much in denial was I that I had somehow believed the star was made with a Sharpie? It was a tattoo.

A tattoo on my sixteen-year-old, too-young-to-get-a-tattoo child. Also no one had permission for a tattoo. (And who puts a tattoo on an underage child?) I wish I could say I took a deep breath and strategically planned how to deal with this situation. Instead, I did this: "Oh my, child! Is that a tattoo? Where did you get it? What were you thinking? Don't you know you have marked your body *forever*?"

To my credit I held back from adding, "And it looks like a monkey did it!"

She looked me in the eye and said, "Mom, it's no big deal. Carol's friend was giving tattoos from the back of his van when we were in the Walmart parking lot. I knew if I asked, you would say no, so I just went for it."

(Please note, this is the child I previously mentioned who later let me know that she calculated punishment versus reward for all decisions in her teenage world and often thought things like this were worth a little grounding or getting her phone taken away. In finding this out, I didn't know whether I should be horrified or proud.)

This was the moment when I should have taken a breath but instead went ahead and lost my mind. We were at the lake cottage, so my hair had already lost it in the humidity and was horrifyingly big and looked flat-out bananas. My eyes were wide, and I held my breath. My kid looked at me like she knew exactly what was coming, and she was not wrong. She finally looked a little bit scared yet still a touch defiant. Before I could even stop myself, I let her have it, just like she knew I would.

"You did *what*? Oh my gosh, you might have a *disease*! Blood poisoning! Hepatitis! What were you thinking? You clearly weren't, and you cannot be trusted. I cannot even let you out of my sight! You are so grounded, kid. Did you hear me? *Grounded!* FOR ALL OF THE DAYS. Do not ask to do a thing. You are going nowhere! And give me that phone. And no TV. I'm not even done with you yet. And you are going to the doctor to be sure you are not going to die of an actual *tattoo*. Argh!"

We stared at each other. I watched as this kid buried her fear under her bravado, looked me dead in the eye, and said to me as if I were the crazy person in the situation, "Gosh, Mom. You don't have to freak out so much. Whatever."

The word *whatever* said in just this tone did nothing to help my mood. I continued to act indeed like the crazy one in this situation.

"Whatever? *Whatever?* I want to know what you have to say for yourself. *What do you have to say?* Explain yourself! Now! I want to know! I mean, what could you possibly say? What reason could you have? But I want to hear it! Now! I cannot believe it! What? What is the *reason?*"

Well, as you can imagine, nothing gets a teenager talking about their heart and motivations quite like a parent screaming in their face like a lunatic. It was also a nice touch that I asked questions without giving her space to answer while also letting her know I thought she was an idiot, so who cared what she said. This moment ended with the child heading off to her room and slamming the door while I seethed and worried and called our pediatrician, whose reward will be long in the land after dealing with my crazy family.

The kid I knew seemed to have disappeared, and in her place was a stranger who seemed to not like me very much and who made very, very questionable choices.

What You Can't Do

You cannot focus on what you are losing or lean into fear. The moments when you are looking at all that is no longer there are the hardest. Especially when you are focusing on the worst parts of having a teenager. You cannot stay in the past, but man, it's tempting. These moments caught me so completely off guard, and the grief I felt over the loss of my small, curly-haired little buddy threatened to leave me completely undone. How was a person so deep in this kind of grief supposed to think clearly and rationally and act as if everything was okay and was just the natural way of the world?

Well, at that moment, I couldn't pretend it was all right. I was miserable, and I kept trying to hold on to what was. I would lie on the couch and dream of the series of kisses she used to give me each time she left the house, and I would feel my heart breaking again and again. I leaned right into this sadness and wallowed in it within my soul. (I am an excellent wallower.)

In reality, that little girl I longed for was still sitting on her same childhood bed. But now the door was closed, so I couldn't see she was also sometimes miserable, unsure of who she was becoming. And instead of her mom pulling up alongside her to let her know it would all be okay? Well, with every reaction, her mom was assuring her that her growing up was terrible and that she was messing it all up. It was all a tragedy.

I stubbornly tried to hold on to the past, to keep her safe and tucked away, and she stubbornly tried to keep doing the work of pulling away and growing up. One day when I was yelling at her about something, I looked at her face—really looked—and saw utter defeat there, together with a little fear and a whole bunch of sadness. My heart broke in a million pieces when I realized I was the cause of most of what I was seeing in her eyes.

I thought again of that little girl, and I could now see the little and big versions of my baby layered on top of each other: The girl in the princess dress staring out from behind the girl with the tattoo and newly dyed hair. The one who loved me like I was the best person on the planet and the one who wished I would just get out of her way so she could *live*. And in all of that, I could see I was hurting her by holding on so tightly to my fear of everything that could happen as she grew.

I knew I never again wanted to cause the look I saw on her face. In my fear of change I was refusing to see her. I needed to remember that I had not lost my girl. She was right there. And if I didn't spend some time getting to know this version of her instead of longing for a past version, I would lose her completely. Because who wants to stay connected to a person who is focused on all the things you no longer are or are doing wrong?

What You Can Do

You can pray, focus on connection, and notice the good. I prayed so many prayers. So. Many. Prayers. You can always, always pray.

I could almost hear God whispering in my ear that I needed to get a grip. I had to work very, *very* hard to let go of my fear. I needed to do a little repair for the things I had already done and said, and I needed to talk *with* her instead of *at* her. I needed to get to know who she was becoming and find all the ways this version of her was also wonderful.

And she *is* wonderful.

And when we mess up, we can reconnect. I got pretty deep in the weeds at first, so my reconnection with the tattooed lady didn't happen overnight. One thing that helped pull me into a better place was tapping into my teaching brain. I pulled out this little thing we in the biz like to call "*notice and name.*" This is simply noticing what you see your kids doing and naming it in a positive, building-up way.

It looks something like this: Let's say your child has decided to plan the world's best outfit, and as a result, everything they own is all over the floor. You might say, "I see the way you love fashion. Your outfit turned out so great [*noticing*]. You are so creative and fun [*naming*]." You are looking for the positive things, the good ways they are already showing up in the world. You are helping them claim a beautiful and true identity.

You may also note this sounds a thousand times better than "You'd better clean that up when you are done," which would have been my old go-to when I wasn't looking at her with the most generous interpretation. "You'd better clean this up" notices the mess and names the flaw—not an identity that is helpful or connecting. We can spend so much time focusing on the wrong things and missing the gift that each kid is. And if she indeed forgot to clean up (let's face it, that's likely), I learned to just gently remind her like I would for a friend instead of making it a huge deal. This was a major shift for me.

I used this noticing and naming to remind both myself and her of all the good and positive things she brought to the world. I bit my tongue as hard as I could whenever I could, not lecturing her about outfits or friends or any of it. And the more I looked at her this way, the more I saw it all a little differently.

You can notice and name all the things with all the people. "You stick by your friends through so many things. You are a really loyal friend." Or "You are an amazing brother. You spend all this time with Sam, and it is so important to him." The things we name become their identity. The way I had been doing it as a nagging, worried mom was creating an identity of failure in my kids. *You are late. You are lazy. You do not follow the rules.*

We gave our girl the identity of capable problem solver by pulling her in to help decide how our relationship would run and what would happen if she broke our trust or violated a boundary. She also helped set what those boundaries were. Like what should happen when you go behind your parents' backs and get a tattoo in some van when you are underage. This still needed to be dealt with, and surprisingly she agreed it was not her smartest moment. Together we decided what tighter guardrails she needed for a while. Our teenagers *want* boundaries, and they also want to have some control over their lives. Negotiating together is so helpful here.

But instead of taking it as a personal attack when she broke the rule, now we focused on helping her figure out what she could have done differently or what she would do to repair the situation. She bore the consequence like all of us do in life when we zig where we should have zagged. We celebrated small wins.

As we focused on working together, we found our joy again. Learning to know the teenage version of your child happens in all the small things—taking a trip to Starbucks, walking through the mall looking for new shoes to fit growing feet, washing dishes together after dinner, or sitting together watching *The Office* on a loop before bed. When you are connected, these things are easier and more fun.

It was in these moments with each of my people that I could get to know their world. Asking which class was their favorite instead of asking how they were doing in classes. Asking whether they had a teacher who inspired them or what the best lunch option was in the cafeteria. Just being genuinely interested in their daily lives. It meant going in gently and with curiosity instead of judgment. And it meant not taking personally any "I don't feel like talking" comments or grunts instead of answers, because despite your best efforts this will still happen.

The only way to connect with them is to stay open and really listen. God placed this exact child in your family for you to know and love forever. He made them to grow and change and become the person they were meant to be. He wants the same thing for us; He wants us to grow and change and become the people we are meant to be, right alongside these children. As they grow and change, we need to as well. And we need to keep our eyes on His creation—these blessed babies He loves even more than we do.

What Happened for Us

We figured it out and never had a single problem with our teens again.

Ha! I kid.

I think this next story sort of sums up what happened for us, and it's a doozy because it involves teens and driving—clearly one of the hardest things we have to experience as parents. I mean, we let a kid strap into a giant hunk of metal that can go more than eighty miles per hour, and then we hand over the wheel and tell them to go with God? It makes no sense to me at all.

Yet we do it. One particular day I picked up a kid from work and then bravely let her drive us home. She navigated the short drive, pulling into our driveway with seeming ease. I was feeling good about myself and about her. *Maybe this won't be so bad,* I thought. Out loud I said, "You did amazing! Way to go, kiddo!" She looked at me with a huge smile.

Then she randomly hit the gas instead of the brake and drove straight into the closed garage door.

The huge white door crumpled like a piece of tinfoil. She hit the side of the doorframe, which stopped the car. This was fortunate because the girl never did find the brake.

I sat in shock for thirty seconds, then reached over and put the car in park myself. I got out and walked around to the driver's side. My girl was sitting with her head in her hands, stunned and I'm sure terrified.

"Are you okay?"

"Yes, Mom. I am SO SORRY!" and she burst into tears.

I will forever feel very proud of my reaction. I assured her it was fine; we were both okay. I hugged her for a long, long time and then led her into the house, where she ran to her room.

I grabbed Todd, who followed me outside. Only then did I blurt out, "It was so scary! She had no idea what to do. *Why* are we letting our kids drive?"

I'd spent so much time wondering how we could send them on purpose to get milk and just wave goodbye while also hoping they did not crash. And now here we were. Fears realized.

But I had kept my cool with her. When things suddenly went off the rails, I held on and kept her connected through all of it. This is what it is all about: They need us to let them go yet be there with cool heads and warm hearts when things do not go as planned.

Later she had to own the consequences of her actions. She paid the deductible, which is what we agreed you need to do when you hit buildings with cars. And then back behind the wheel she went, because they have to keep growing up.

Note: After having suffered through the learning experience of the first couple of kids, I now flat-out refuse to ride shotgun. Yes, even after they have that license. I have tapped out. I cannot do all the things well as a mom, and I have decided I'm going to put zero energy into trying to be good at this. We are allowed to wave a white flag now and then, and this is mine. When the fear is overpowering, we can also step away from it.

We have to keep as connected as we can and then let go and live like they will be just fine. It is hard to do, but we have to let them go *anyway*.

The Good News

I wasn't sure how I found myself full circle, now sitting in a tattoo/piercing parlor with my fifteen-year-old, but here we were.

Kate had been begging for a piercing, and when my sister decided to take her girl, she asked, "Would Kate enjoy this too?"

I knew she would. I dug deep. The mom who freaked out at her sister's tattoo years ago and who had also outlawed piercings of all kinds said yes.

Together we sat, picking out her piercing and chatting away. Her sisters had only minimally grumbled that I would never have let *them* do that at her age.

Sometimes we need to let go of the rules and focus on the human. We show them that they are still seen and that they matter. So sometimes we will find ourselves dropping everything to get them to a piercing parlor. Who would have thought it?

There are so many ways we need to get to know and understand our newly minted teenagers. (And it doesn't even have to involve piercing.) A lot of it will be familiar: You will be feeding them around the clock, and you won't be getting a lot of sleep because they are up until all hours. And the new parts? Well, these nearly grown humans are full of fun, humor, and joy in so many moments that you will be able to glimpse the adult friendship that could be yours right around the corner. They will get your jokes and be fun to take on trips (mostly). You will wake up in the morning to a dance party in your kitchen and a stack of pancakes made just for you. You might even be able to steal their shoes, and you have built-in tech support under your roof. And when things are not so fun? I promise that you can handle every bit of it.

Long Story Short

- Our babies are right there in our big kids. Remember to look at all the good in front of you and *tell them* what you love about them getting older so they don't think you only long for their littleness.

- Our kids will do dumb things and break the rules, but we need to stay calm, smart, sane, and regulated.

- Notice and name the good you see in them. Assume they are doing the best they can.

- Prayer and therapy both help.

- Find ways to connect with your kids by learning about and listening to their passions. Just like when you watched *Dora the Explorer* on a loop, you may now have to follow weird people on TikTok and learn about cars.

Dear God,

Please give me the strength to be the one who remains calm and the one who reaches out. Please let me overcome my pride and apologize to my kids when I wrong them. Grant me patience for every tattoo and weird haircut and piercing.

Also let me stop yelling. Silence my tongue. Let Your words come from my mouth and not mine. Put Your holy hand over my mouth lest I send my child into the well of sadness. Let me remember their brains are growing and changing as much as their bodies, so this is why they seem a little crazy. And this is why they are amazing, creative problem solvers. Help me appreciate that, even when they are trying to creatively problem solve their way out of cleaning their rooms.

Help me notice and name the good in them, and help me listen to all their ideas about cars and fashion even when it is past my bedtime.

Amen.

CHAPTER 3

Communication and Connection

When to Try to Talk to Them and
When to Just Give Up and Text

I walked down the stairs and knocked on her door like it was a regular morning. I had no idea it wasn't. I didn't know that sometime in the night the kid behind that door had had her heart broken into a million pieces.

I said, "Hey, kiddo! Time to get up! We are doing an awesome family breakfast this morning."

She answered with a text: *Mom, Greg and I broke up last night. I am not coming out today. I don't need anything. I'll be okay. I just don't want to talk to anyone.*

And what was I supposed to do with that? I wanted to barge in and hug my kid and yell at Greg. Or maybe hug him too. Who knew what was happening here.

But I could do *zero* of those things.

I did try to get my foot wedged into that very closed door and say something to help. Because of course I didn't yet believe my child when she said that words wouldn't help and that she didn't want to hear them.

"Can I bring you food? Your dad? Are you sure you don't want to talk?"

Mom, I'm fine. Please leave, she texted.

"Okay, but I need to hear your voice," I said.

"It's okay, Mom. Now go."

I went. But my heart was breaking, and that awesome family breakfast suddenly felt like the absolute last thing in the world I wanted to do. I wanted to fix my kid's heart.

I wanted to burst through that wall of privacy. I longed to scour social media and all her texts to find out how she was doing. But these were hidden from me with the stealth of a grade A spy. I had to face facts and realize this kid was miserable and I wasn't getting in. I could see her misery. I swear I could feel it in my mom bones. And I had words that I felt would help her heal and move forward. But parenting teenagers sometimes means giving them more space than we want to.

I gave space, then broke down and tried to give words. I heard over and over again, "Mom, I will be fine. I just need to be alone."

I had to face the hard truth: I couldn't fix it. Instead, we all lived through some miserable weeks. This was the first big heartbreak in our family, so it was the hardest. We were sad and afraid for her. We couldn't know that behind that closed door, this child was working through it and eventually would open the door and rejoin the world. And of course she didn't want to talk about it even then. Trust me, I asked. A lot. Eventually I had to accept that this was my kid's way of dealing with things and that it was very different from mine.

When she finally did come out of it, I heard some hard

truths. She was very honest about how my pushing actually made things worse. (Side note: When kids are very sad or hiding out, we also need to monitor their mental health and make sure they know when to reach out for help—hence my checking.) I didn't yet know how this kid would work through things. It was a whole year later when she finally told me what had happened to initiate this heartbreak.

It is so hard to get used to pulling back and waiting and listening, isn't it? Especially because there was a time when everyone wanted a piece of us.

Back in the day of parenting five littles, I often ended the day feeling like there was never enough of me to go around. I would plop down on the couch in utter exhaustion after making the food, cleaning up the food, and navigating the daily "they got the blue/red/pink cup yesterday" thing, and I would be flat-out done. But they were not. They all still wanted to sit by me and talk to me and tell me all the things. So. Many. Stories.

I remember grabbing a bag of Doritos one afternoon, sneaking upstairs to my room like some sort of lunatic, locking my door and sitting up against it for good measure, and then texting my husband to say that I thought my ears were actually bleeding from so many sounds coming in. I was touched out. Peopled out. But even when I hid, they would find me, and soon little fingers were poking under the door while a little voice said, "Mommmmmyyyyy . . . I neeeeed youuuuu." (It is no mistake that my original blog was named Hiding in the Closet with Coffee.)

And then, just when I thought I wouldn't make it through another Minecraft story or round of Barbies, it turned out I didn't have to. All at once, it seemed, they stopped talking. They stopped saying, "Look at me!" and started saying, "MOM, stop looking at me. Geez!" All of my people were suddenly just beyond reach, behind their bedroom doors, locked in relationships with their phones that held a million text threads to all the people they were chatting with all day long.

It shouldn't have shocked me that this kid didn't want to spill her guts about a breakup.

What You Can't Do

You cannot force them to talk. Darn it all. Some days I would pick them up from school and those kids who used to fight over talking to me barely grunted in my direction. I remember one day when I picked them up from the middle and high schools and tried to start up a conversation. I tried all the tricks, asking questions about their day (which is really the most boring thing you can ask them), about the song on the radio, or whether they wanted to put on Spotify. I was asking what their plans were for the night and what they wanted for dinner (I was grasping) when finally one of them put me out of my misery. "Mom, it's nothing personal, but we really just don't want to talk to you after school. Maybe later, okay?"

Welp, that was a nice little hit of honesty. The other heads in the van nodded in agreement, and my son even gave me a little sympathy pat on the shoulder as he put in his earbuds. He felt sorry for me. *I am suddenly the one on the outside they all feel bad for? Like, poor Mom; let's just humor her? Hey, I used to hide from you, kid.* But to be fair, I felt pretty bad for myself. I watched them text their friends as they chuckled out loud here and there at some conversation I wasn't a part of, and I felt really, really old. And alone.

Even though I knew I was no longer their go-to for many things, I was trying mightily to keep my foot in the door of their worlds. But what was this tomfoolery? *Why don't you want to talk to me? I'm fun! I have good stories! And why can't you just tell me about your day, kid? NOTHING happened at school? I need to stop asking you things? You don't want to even say a single sentence to your mom who listened to your stories about Pokèmon battles for years? Got it.* Picture me standing in the kitchen holding a Wii controller and a dream of getting this tall kid to play one more round of Lego Star Wars with me. But he had gone on to the Xbox with his buddies. Both the Wii and I were old news. Sadness.

Oh, how the tables had turned. Who had I become? Who had they become? And how was I going to figure out how to connect with these tall versions of my babies who were no longer inviting me into their worlds?

The answer was that I wouldn't be automatically invited like I was before. I couldn't force my way in. But that didn't mean they didn't want or need me. It was just going to look different. Those teen brains were growing and changing, and as a result they needed space to sort out their thoughts. And their first instinct was to connect with their friends and push away from their parents.

We might have to get over ourselves here. Many parents may be thinking, *Man, you don't want me around? Fine. Have it your way*—or feeling really sad or thinking they did something wrong.

You didn't. It isn't personal. Knowing that this phase of life is not only emotional but also biological can help us make better plans for how to get our kids to talk and how to listen now that they are no longer crawling into our laps to tell us about everything.

My teens needed a lot less talking and advice from me, but they still needed *me*, just on some different terms—theirs.

What You Can Do, Part One

What you can do is really hard, at least for me. You can be *quieter.* Yup. I know. I got pretty sad about not giving all the advice. I love to talk, and giving advice is my jam. But I needed to learn to shut up, which is hard when I have really wise things to say. For one of my people, it was absolutely key that I said no words. I could offer ideas sparingly and at just the right intervals. A friend of mine said she had to learn not to ask questions, because questions drove her teenager mad. Another had to learn to love going to the mall because that is where her kid opened up. She hated the mall with a passion, but her kiddo loved it and would talk there, so to the mall she went. If we want to keep those lines of communication open, we have to follow our kids' lead and lean into what they know and love.

A big part of this parenting-teenagers gig is just making ourselves available. It reminds me of the feeling I had at dances in high school, milling around waiting for a boy to notice me and ask me to dance. It's so tricky. And just at the point in life when you start wanting to go to bed earlier, they will want to spill their guts around midnight on a school night. Prop those eyelids open with toothpicks, and take advantage of the opportunity to listen up. My boy became so elusive as a teen that now when I hear him come home from work, I drop what I am doing and run to the main floor. I try to get a few words in and a nice hug while he grabs a snack before he disappears into the basement.

These days if my tall kids look in my direction and move their mouths like they might say something, I don't move a muscle. I do not want to spook them. I don't even really make eye contact. Either I just wait, or if the mood seems right, I say something really chill like "How's it going?" and hope for some sort of answer. I busy myself in some way until the conversation is really going, then sit down and listen with all my might. The trick to keeping the conversation going is giving the right responses.

These cannot be invasive or contain any kind of judgment

whatsoever. If you are *too* interested, they might stop talking. And if they get even a whiff of an opinion they haven't asked for, you are done. For some kids, even if they ask for an opinion, you might need to hold back until they have asked a few times and then make sure your opinion is very light and leaves a lot of room for them to think about it.

They need to start working things out for themselves. Pulling back on sharing *all* our own thinking gives them the chance to be the ones who do the thinking and deciding—something they desire. We are just there to guide and coach, not to tell them exactly what to do, which is so easy to say and so hard to do when we can see exactly how they should move forward. For them to become independent, they need to practice being independent. We are there to support, not to give directions.

We need to give our kids space and privacy and then a wide-open door to tell us what's on their minds. Sometimes they will open their own doors and invite you in, ask your opinion, and maybe even share about what is happening. Take advantage of these moments! You cannot force them to happen, so when they do, you need to be prepared. Have a little nonjudgmental advice at the ready.

Their invitation is key. When you have something to say, you need to ask yourself whether the door is open. If it is not, do not say the things. This will save you endless amounts of conflict and grief. If your teenager doesn't want to talk, you need to respect that boundary. If you try to deliver the lecture through their closed door, I promise you they are not listening and will not be likely to open the door anytime soon.

It can be so frustrating when you are *full* of wisdom and nobody wants to hear it. I can picture one of my kids sitting in front of me with his eyes glazed over while I went on and on about why he shouldn't hold on to a relationship that was hurting him. I had so many good reasons! I was so wise! I could see this wouldn't end well! So, why was he not listening to me?

He couldn't hear me because the door to his mind was closed. I was screaming at nothing. He was passing time until he could just get away from me. But when I learned to wait for that opening, I knew there was a small but significant chance he would hear my wisdom.

Playing your cards right with teenagers is pretty much like walking through a field filled with land mines, but it *can* be done. You *can* do this. You may have to fight every instinct in your body (I do this on the regular), and you might even have to rehearse so you are ready for that open-door moment.

Here is where the power of prayer will serve you well. If an open-door moment came on with my kids and I wasn't ready, I would stop and throw up a giant prayer to God that He would give me the words I needed. *Speak through me, please, God. Give me the words to make him believe he is worthy of better. Amen.*

What You Can Do, Part Two

When it is time to speak, you can be mindful with your words. No matter what the situation, the words you use are important. As an educator I have spent years thinking about and experimenting with asking the right question or giving the right nudge and response to get kids to think about a problem or an issue. All that practice paid off as my kids hit the teen years. I worked hard on my language, and over time I learned some key phrases we can count on when we are trying to be good listeners and communicators with our kids.

Here are things you can say to your teens that may open them up:

- Wow!

- Say more about that.

- That sounds so interesting!

- What happened next?

- How did that turn out?

- Do you have any feelings about that?

- What do you think you should do next?

- Do you want some advice about that?
  (Judgment call here.)

- I love listening to you!

Responses that may be conversation shutdowns include these:

- I don't think you should have said that.

- I don't think you should have done that.

- I'm so worried now.

- You must be mad/sad/glad/etc. (This is called "assuming their feelings.")

- You really should have done x/y/z instead.

- You are going to need to do x/y/z next.

- We need to talk. (They hate this one; it makes them feel like doom is coming.)

- I'm so disappointed in you.

And if your teenager has gone silent in all the ways, there are still a few things you can do to nudge them forward.

Once again, you might just need to give them time. And if not, we have the blessing and curse that is texting. It is an actual gift in the land of parenting. Our kids will sometimes say things to us over text that they cannot manage to say aloud. And they are used to texting their friends, so it is like we are working with their native language. You can often use texting to find out the boy they like or to get them to bring you something from the kitchen. I call this a win-win.

Then there will be times when sit-down, drag-out, look-in-the-eyeballs conversations are necessary. We reserve these for times when kids are really in the weeds or we as a family need to deal with an issue. We set the tone for talking and listening, saying as little as necessary to communicate our points, then letting them talk while we listen without judgment or jumping in.

Writing these words is super easy, but if you were in my home this week, you would be saying, "Amy, you really need to work on that, friend. I just watched how you dealt with the whole 'no one is getting up on time this summer or helping with anything' thing, and you were a hot mess." And you would be correct. I strive for this and fail way too often. But I don't stop striving, and my kids try to keep me on point because we talk about talking. I let them know that I am trying to respect their space and their thinking but that I might sometimes fail, and they have the right to ask for what they need from me when it comes to how we communicate and connect with one another.

And know, when the lines of communication are open, you will also hear some hard things from your kids—sometimes things you'll wish you didn't hear. Right under my roof this has happened. I have walked into bedrooms and found crying people who have hugged me and whispered in my ears the things that were on their hearts, and sometimes these things have taken my breath away.

These are their stories to hold close and are not mine to share. So, dear reader, this is where you take my place—but in your house, not mine—in a teenager's messy room or on your own bed. You thought you would be sleeping, but instead there was a knock on the door and your arms are now around one of your dear children. Your ears hear their hardest things. Your heart cracks open, and their pain floods your veins.

But they have trusted you, and you are there. And then we *know* what we know. Even if we cannot say it aloud, we know. It is so hard. But it is also so good. They have chosen to tell us and to let us be right there in their stories. That is the gift. We cannot run from the beautiful, brutal moments. Instead, we remind ourselves we are one of our child's best guides on this journey, and we stay with them in love and grace for all the minutes. When we are connected to our kids, we get the honor of helping them with their hardest things.

What Happened for Us

I was driving down the road listening to the *SmartLess* podcast, chuckling along with Jason, Will, and Sean and innocently thinking about what I was going to make for dinner. We were on our way to a routine doctor appointment, and my child was on his phone as per usual. Out of the blue he set his phone down and started talking. He asked a direct question about a significant thing I had been unaware of only seconds before, and I froze. I had to make a quick 180-degree turn in my mind because suddenly the door swung wide open.

This kid took me up on the whole "you can tell me anything" thing. It was time to address a giant issue. Time to say a prayer and remember I was so lucky that he was talking. In these moments, God has given me so many good words I never would have thought of on my own. I now recommend clinical-strength deodorant because you never know when a big moment that will make you sweat is going to come.

We had a great ten-minute conversation. Regrettably, I kept trying to rekindle it over the next few weeks until he asked, "Are you going to keep bringing this up forever?" I got the picture.

"Absolutely not. I am so sorry. But I do reserve the right to check in on this like maybe once a month. Fair?"

He rolled his eyes but also answered, "Fair." They want and need us to check in and be interested—just not all the time. And only on their terms. *Got it.*

So, while the moments your kids want you are now fewer and farther between, they still pack enough of a punch to exhaust you just like the constant "Mom, look at me" moments did. Good times.

The Good News

The most powerful tools we have in these hard times are at our fingertips at a moment's notice: love and prayer. We can share with God what is on our hearts. We need to sit in the quiet and listen and lean into God's whispers. We have to do so much listening. But when I have really listened to my heart, God has provided me with things to say that had to come from Him, because I knew they were better than anything I ever could have come up with. As words have come out of my mouth, I knew God was behind me. He loves our kids even more than we do. He wants to help us help them. We just have to stop and breathe and listen.

There have been times when one of my kids was so lost and so scared. And I was so lost and so scared. As we know, that is not our best parenting place. These are the moments when we must lean on God, the divine parent. He understands with a love that surpasses anything our humanness can conceive of. He has given me the words and the courage to lead my children out of the darkness, as He takes my hand and leads me out as well. He wants to help us through the little things, but man, does He come through with the big ones too. And I'm pretty sure He crawls up on my bed and holds me in His arms so I can tell Him all my own problems while also holding my now-tall baby who is telling me hers. What a gift.

You will truly be right there in it with them. In all the ways. And I believe that God has given us these children for just this reason: to be their champions through all of it. *All* of it. We can do it. I will make it, and you will too.

Long Story Short

- They need you as much as they did when they were small, even if they are not always talking.

- Give them space when they need it. Yes, you have to.

- Be ready when they do come to you; give some thought to what you might say or do so you can choose your words carefully.

- Use technology when words are hard. GIFs work in a pinch.

- Respect their privacy, and try not to stalk their technology.

- Pray for the right words; let God speak to your heart so you can speak to theirs.

Dear God,

Please draw our kids close to us. Give us the words we need to continue to teach them all that we can. Help me keep my mouth shut when I need to and to really and truly listen to what they have to say, hearing their thoughts in my mind and in my heart. Give me strength when I do not agree with what they are saying, and help me give them space to make their own choices and mistakes. Help me know when it is time to give them stricter guardrails and how to balance this with keeping them open to coming to me with their issues.

Let me step into Your footsteps, thinking about how You parent us with all the love. Let me find all the ways to help them hear me, and let me refrain from losing my mind when they just do not see the wisdom I am offering. (I have such wisdom, don't I, Lord?)

Anyway, keep me from fear, and let the fruits of my labor be found in kids who love to come home and tell me all the things, even the hard ones—even when they are old and gray and I am older and grayer. I want to love them for all time.

Amen.

CHAPTER 4

Parenting the First Teenager in Your House

Making That First Pancake and Hoping for the Best

I found the contraband right as he was getting ready to walk out the door for school. In all fairness, the kid in question had asked for help in finding his computer charger and had left the forbidden item almost in plain sight—on the bed next to a few school papers and an empty water bottle tipped on its side. I couldn't miss it. I was not being a snoop . . . at least not this time.

I couldn't even deal with the fact we were going down this path again. Same problem, different kid. And because it was a different kid and a few years had passed, my reaction to the whole situation was swift and decisive.

I didn't miss a beat.

I held the vape up with one hand and put my work backpack on at the same time. (I can even multitask in a crisis because I am a mom—I know you know exactly what I mean.) I looked at the kid in question and asked, "What is this, kid, and just *why?*"

Said child stopped in his tracks with a deer-in-the-headlights look in his eyes. He glanced down at his phone and back up at me, and I could see him calculating his next move.

I looked right back at him, staring him down because I felt ready for what was coming next. "Really, kiddo. *Why?* You cannot have this in our house. What is going on? I really just need to know so we can help you." I looked into those eyes I knew so well, and I didn't waver.

Calm. Measured. And somehow still walking kids to the door because it was time to go.

For a million little reasons, this child was able to look at me and come clean about what I had found and why he had it in the first place.

We talked about why he was even using this, how bad it was, and how there were other ways of dealing with anxiety. We talked about how hard it might be to quit and what needed to happen next. I had been through this before. I knew. Said child agreed as we all got into the car and another child realized she forgot her water bottle and ran back in for it. While we waited, we formed a plan that was acceptable to all parties concerned. This child may have also looked a little like he couldn't believe this all had happened.

We drove to school, he got out of the car, and I said "I love you" to all my people—and also that I was throwing the vape away and to please not even try and tell me they were expensive because I cared about that zero percent.

School drop-off was completed.

This is the value of being the second, third, fourth, or fifth pancake. You often get the mother who has been through it already, who knows what works and what doesn't, and who can move past her emotional response to one that is more logical, actionable, and actually helpful. This is not the mother the first pancake enjoyed.

He told me later this made all the difference to him when he got his third (yes, third) speeding ticket. He was able to come home and let us help him deal with it instead of "speeding off a cliff." And nothing could have made my heart happier. Unless it was no speeding ticket at all.

When my firstborn heard the story about the vape, she replied, "Man, I slithered on the ground on my stomach so these kids could sprint."

She wasn't wrong.

Because she was the first pancake. You know, like when you're making pancakes and use that first one to figure out whether you have to adjust the batter or the heat. And after you figure the adjustments out, all the other pancakes come out fluffier and more even because the testing with the first one happened.

That first pancake teaches you things, and you do better after that.

And man, my first pancake taught me so many things.

She remembers a similar scene that didn't include a calm mom. It involved a yelling, angry mom, and the whole thing didn't end at school drop-off. Instead, there were tears and slamming doors and a giant grounding—all of which did little to deal with the problem or make it go away. I hadn't yet learned that my yelling and anger pushed my child away from me and closed down any line of communication that might have helped us move forward.

The first pancake didn't always get that reasonable, non-judgmental, calm parent. Because that parent hadn't yet learned that it would be okay, that she couldn't control everything, and that loving your child by filling them with your fears didn't really get you anywhere. Everything you go through with that first teenager is so fraught with emotion, mostly because you are still a little bit baffled that you have a teenager at all. Baffled isn't our best place to parent from. But we learn from it, and so do our kids, and we comfort ourselves in knowing that there are no perfect parents.

Fortunately, we can regroup and make new decisions. And the best place to start is the good old-fashioned apology. I, unfortunately, did not use this advice as liberally as I should have the first time around. I just kept the temperature on that burner too high and cried that my pancake was burning, quite certain it was the pancake's fault! In the end I had to face the fact that I was the only one who could turn down the heat and stop the burn.

It took me a while to get there.

If you are parenting your first pancake, you will need to move from that baffled, emotional place as quickly as you can. It is impossible to prepare for every situation your teenager will throw at you, so don't even try. But you can begin now to think about how to control your emotions and reactions. You can't necessarily help what your teen is going to do, but you can control how you react.

And if you are parenting your only teenager, do not get stressed out that your first pancake is your only pancake. You've got this, friend. I promise. And you can learn from my mistakes. I've adjusted the heat and batter for you.

What We Can't Do

We cannot parent from our emotions in the moment. If I could have a do-over, I would sit down and make a list of what kind of parent I want to be and then carry that list around with me for when times are hard. I would put wonderful things on that list like *Be forgiving, understanding, and a good listener; set solid boundaries; and be intentional.*

Because I was flying by the seat of my pants, I became a reactor instead of an actor in any given situation. So the list of how I started out parenting that first pancake looked more like *Be a worrier, the queen of the long lecture, anxious, a rule maker, a rule an enforcer, the authority, and one who wings it.* I really, really like the other list better. But, I remind myself, I was baffled and emotional and not my best self, and my teenager was also baffled and emotional and not her best self, so it all became sort of a mess pretty quickly.

Being an authority figure who is winging it is never a good thing. And being worried and anxious did not help either of us. My long lectures fell on deaf ears, leading to the saying "Rules are made to be broken" being tattooed on my kid's heart.

Because I wasn't being intentional, I was parenting from a place of worry and grief. Yet constantly looking backward made me miss what was in front of me. One of the worst dangers of this type of parenting is that it sends our teenagers the message that we liked the younger versions of them better. This message, from the ones who are supposed to love them unconditionally, comes at a time when they are already doubting so much about themselves.

They desperately need us to cheer them on and help them discover and appreciate their new selves too. They need us to get excited that they can get all their own food, that they can have friends over and we don't need to do a thing except supply snacks and stay (mostly) away, and that they can drive themselves to the store to get us milk.

What We Can Do

We can work on our own emotional reactions as they grow so we can show up for them in the way they need us to.

Think about all the firsts you had with this pancake that were incredible: first word, first steps, first food, first playdate. Most likely you documented and celebrated each of these. As subsequent pancakes arrived, you loved them just as much.

However, their firsts were now *expected* and didn't have the element of surprise like the first kid's—and even the documentation of their accomplishments might have waned.

It's similar when your first teenager reaches milestones: first day of high school, first dance, first love interest. And because they are teenagers, they might have other milestones that certainly don't deserve celebrating but are nonetheless unforgettable: first time getting pulled over for speeding, first time lying about their location, first time breaking curfew, first time slamming their door in your face.

Many of us are not prepared to deal with any of it this first time around. We are no more equipped than when we brought them home from the hospital and needed to figure out how to feed them, change them, and get them to sleep through the night. We might think we will be cool under pressure, but the first time that child looks you in the eyes and lies to you about something pretty big, you will be some weird combination of heartbroken, enraged, and paralyzed with not knowing how on earth to deal with it.

If we have imagined something like this might happen and have thought about our reactions, we will be better prepared. I did not do this. Instead, I did things like cry (not effective), yell (also not effective), and throw out random punishments I couldn't always enforce, like "That's it! You are *never* leaving this house again!" (really, really not effective).

You, friend, will be in the prepared category because you are reading this book and will be armed and ready to stay calm, cool, and collected. By the way, taking a deep breath can be a great first step. Here is also where I like to close my eyes and say a quick prayer:

> Dear God above,
>   Let me not kill this sweet child with words. Remind me that I cannot ground her for life. Please

give me the strength to stay calm and treat her like our dear child that she is. Also, please give me the words (the non-yelling kind) to help her see that lying to me is never a great plan. Hold us in the palm of Your hand, Lord, and flick me gently in the forehead if I start to lose my cool. Amen.

If you feel like even with the Lord's help in this moment you have nothing but a huge emotional reaction, it is okay to tell your dear offspring that you need a minute to collect yourself. This can be good for both of you, as long as you don't inadvertently terrify your child. You will need to say something like "I'm having some big feelings right now that I don't want to put on you. They are mine to deal with, so I'm going to need a few minutes to think, and then we can talk."

With the first pancake I may have said something like "I cannot even look at you right now. I am so mad. I need to calm down, and then I will deal with you." *Ouch.* It's hard for me to even read that, let alone write it. Words matter so much, and we need to choose them carefully.

Try to keep the emotion to a minimum (your teen will have plenty for both of you), be clear and calm, know what kind of boundaries you need to set and name them (or ask for time to think and circle back instead of just saying anything), and give both of you a lot of grace. A. Lot. Of. Grace.

What Happened for Us

I still spontaneously apologize to my first pancake for random things. When I am sitting with my fourth pancake watching movies on the couch and I think about how it is all so much easier, I know some of that has to do with this kid but some of it has to do with me. I am different. I am more relaxed, more open to her ideas about her life, less concerned with how it all looks, and more confident that it will be okay and that we can weather the challenges. I owe this in large part to that first pancake.

I'll be sitting in this ease, and a memory of something I said or did when dealing with pancake one will make me cringe. I'll find myself getting up from the couch and walking randomly into her room to say things like "I'm so sorry I grounded you so much." Or "I've been thinking a lot about how I didn't really listen to you when you were a teenager. I was just so afraid because I love you so much. I'm sorry I wasn't different."

She usually looks up from where she is sitting cross-legged on her bed, computer in her lap, earphones now hanging around her neck, laughs, and asks, "What made you think of *that*?"

I know she forgives me, but I also know I have to be consistent with how I treat her as we forge new pathways in our relationship now that she is a young adult. I am always working to be a little better today than I was yesterday.

A few years ago we had a moment in the car that let me know she was thinking about it too. And her comments summed it right up.

"We are so much better, Mom. I think it's because you've finally learned to let go a bit more."

I held my breath.

She continued, "And I think I've finally learned it's okay to hold on."

Yes.

The more she had tried to pull away, the harder I had held on. And the harder I held on, the harder she tried to pull away, until my grip on her and her strength in trying to escape had almost ripped us each in two. I'm so lucky it didn't, and I'm so grateful for the healing.

The Good News

Have you ever read a book where a character gives birth, instantly falls in love with the baby, and vows to take care of this baby and to be everything for them? And then have you ever read a book where the mother of a teenager is the person who just exists to be tolerated? Or even avoided? These plots play themselves out over and over in real life.

I have always wondered how the mother goes from being the person who was that baby's entire world to being the person that baby will grow up to avoid phone calls from. I decided I never want to be the character in our story that my children are trying to avoid.

I want to hold on to that part of the parent-child relationship that starts the moment you pick up your child for the very first time, when your soul shifts into completeness. I now try to parent in such a way that even my first pancake, the one who arguably got the most mistake-ridden part of me, will want to pick up the phone when I call her when she is thirty. This is the goal, friend.

Long Story Short

- This is the first time you have parented a teenager. Give yourself the same grace you did when you were parenting a newborn.

- Parenting the first pancake is fraught with emotion, and you may feel confused and afraid. That is normal, but do not make parenting decisions based on confusion and fear.

- Long lectures get you nowhere. Random punishments, the same.

- Say you are sorry when you do something you regret, and remind your child you are new to this too. Try to figure it out together when you can.

- It is okay to take a break and regroup to decide intentionally how you want to handle any situation.

- Have fun with their firsts just like you did when they were little.

- Parent in such a way that they will want to call you with their troubles when they are thirty. You do not want to be the mom character all the kid characters are avoiding.

Dear Lord,

I am new at this parenting-teenagers thing, and it is really, really hard. When I have no clue what to do, when this first pancake throws me for yet another loop, and when I am looking at them with no idea what to say, will You please give me the words?

Help me know that even though I cannot see the path in front of me because I haven't walked it yet, a reasonable end is in sight and we will indeed make it to the other side. Send all Your wisdom and patience, Lord, when my kid is testing the boundaries and when I frankly have no idea what the boundaries should be.

Help me see all the good in my kid, this beautiful creation You have sent to us to help raise up and send off into the world. Thank You for this child, Lord. They are everything. My heart is both weary and grateful.

Amen.

CHAPTER 5

I Am Not Parenting Myself

Put This on Repeat or Suffer the Consequences

I was a born rule follower. I listened to my parents and teachers and followed their rules about 83 percent of the time. I was a joiner who wanted nothing more than to be captain of the cheerleaders and president of the student council. I dated polite boys, went to dances, had amazing friends, and loved to have parties where everyone could come because all the parents knew there would be no alcohol under any circumstances. I wanted to get good grades and go to college to be a teacher. And I loved hanging out and playing games with my family on the weekends and going out to eat chicken sandwiches at a local restaurant on Friday nights.

I'm sure I was also an eye-rolling drama queen filled with disaster a bunch of the time and drove my parents crazy with my messy room and penchant for being late to everything. I also was super amazing at starting fights with my sisters over the corded phone that hung on the wall at the bottom of the basement stairs, and the poor sister who had to share a room with me would tell you living next to my devil-may-care attitude when it came to cleaning was certainly no picnic. But mostly my teenage years were uncomplicated and easy.

I brought my teenage self to parenting my teenagers, as we all do whether we mean to or not.

In my case, I thought that all I had to do was parent my own children exactly as my parents parented me and that my children, too, would be rule-following leaders who wanted good grades—and hopefully wanted to hang out with me on the weekends.

But God laughs in the face of our plans sometimes, and this was no exception. The kids who were born to us are rule-breaking, question-asking, pushing-the-boundaries, loud and fun and crazy delights of humans. I'm not even sure they would have said hi to me if we had gone to high school together, honestly. That is how cool they are.

If only I could parent a miniature version of me! How easy that would be!

But that's not what happened. There was crossover, sure—I can see my genes popping up here and there. One kid loves to read, another loves to lead, one has my laugh, and they all really enjoy a super messy bedroom. But mostly I had to completely rearrange the picture I had in my head of what parenting teenagers would be like. My parents laid out the rules, and I followed them. I laid out the rules, and there was a whole lot more breaking of them than I would have ever dreamed of doing.

What We Can't Do

We cannot parent our kids exactly as our moms and dads parented us. And I have amazing parents. The best. So it was baffling when using their exact parenting moves didn't work. I didn't quite get it, so I spent some time trying to force my kids to just *be me*. (Worse, *be me* in the 1980s. I wanted to hang a clipboard, let them sign up for phone time, and know they were spending their Friday nights at the roller rink.)

It, of course, was not to be. I had to navigate plenty of phone fights with my kids, but now these phones were full-on computers that contained the whole world and lived in their pockets. I was unprepared for this different ball game. Not knowing what else to do, I doubled down and kept trying to do the things that worked in my house growing up until I could really look at what was underneath those things. I grabbed on to the parenting moves my own mom and dad used that were focused on love and acceptance. Because for me, under the rules I needed to follow there was always, always love. I knew love was a gift they had given me that I could take forward into this new world. I could parent with love like my parents did; I just needed to do it in a way that spoke to the kids I was raising in the time I was raising them.

Not only did I have to change my mind about the era I was living in, but I also needed to change my philosophy around parenting in this new world of question askers who could also google the answers. I was getting nowhere with the "I say the thing; you do the thing" approach. My kids were so wildly unlike me in this arena.

You may have had a different experience and have been trying to parent in a totally different way than your parents did because your upbringing didn't work well for you or because you have some trauma. There are a million reasons we might need to do things differently for our teenagers. Basing these on love and connection as our filter is my most helpful tool.

What We Can Do

We can genuinely connect with these people we are raising right where they are. Every time I set up a classroom at the beginning of a school year, my whole goal was to get to know the students and to learn what made them *them*. I then found the good in each student and delighted in them. I honestly loved each one and tried to create a place where we were all invested in the community. As a result, we had fewer behavior problems in the classroom, and they also ended the year as a bonded community. It made it hard to see them go because we had become like a little family.

I knew this worked for my students because it is based on tried-and-true educational research and practice. Kids need to have basic needs met and feel safe to be themselves in order to learn. And guess what? It works when parenting our teenagers, too, because it is also based on what humans need: connection—to feel loved, cared about, and seen. I needed to make this the way our world worked at home. I needed to figure out how to be in a relationship with each of my people, find the good, connect us all to one another, and then parent in a way that kept us there together.

I leaned into parenting for relationships. And just like my students, each of my kids needed something a little different (or vastly different), based on who they were born to be. Our "rules" became different according to each person's needs, their wiring, and their particular circumstance.

Having different rules for each kid—at home or in the classroom—doesn't mean it's unfair. I told my students the "broken-leg story" every year: If one of the students were to break their leg, every student wouldn't get a cast on their own leg. Instead, we might have one kid with a cast, another with a paper cut who needed a Band-Aid, and another who didn't need a thing at that moment. Each person would get their needs met, but they should prepare for that to look different.

There simply isn't a rule that works the same for every single kid. We need to look at each kid and each situation and move forward from there. Each of these people is a different human, and we parent accordingly.

What Happened for Us

Embracing a connected approach means things become more individualized and focused on relationship. For one kid, giving choices had always been key. We needed to ask her every night when she was little if she would rather walk or be carried up the stairs. Without this question, she felt out of control and a meltdown ensued. This was who she was. So questions like "Would eleven-thirty or midnight work best for a curfew tonight?" were just as key. Or "Would you like to see your friends on Thursday or Friday night this week?" Or "What do you think is a fair way to handle the fact that we don't agree about your staying out until two o'clock in the morning?" Bringing her to the table and letting her have control diffused many situations and was a great way to build decision-making that she would need as an adult.

Another child was a calm, sleepy baby who I think was trying to please us right out of the gate. She is in tune to the feelings of those around her, so we sometimes need to talk her out of worrying about how her actions will affect others. She needs to think more about herself so she doesn't lose her own hopes and dreams. This kid needed calm, gentle parenting with lots of reassurance so she could learn to listen to her inner voice. Too many choices could be overwhelming to her. We found that laying out clear boundaries helped her and that being too stern would close her down.

This was very different from another one of her counterparts who needed not only to be parented with a gentle approach but also to make his own choices with a side order of saying as few words about any of it as possible. Yet another has her own way of doing things as well as a fear of missing out that is second to none. This had to be considered whenever we were working through something. And our dear baby of the family (who is no longer a baby) usually wants everyone to be happy, so he might need help finding his own needs.

Each kid is different, and therefore we meet their needs differently. Whew! All these kids raised in the same house were not even close to the same. There couldn't be a one-size-fits-all set of rules. If you have more than one child, you might see this as well.

We try to always remember to tell them they are as God made them and we get the amazing pleasure of finding out who God made them to be. And God didn't make them to be us.

He also didn't make them to fulfill our lost dreams and desires. He didn't make them to be something we could be proud of in a way that would show others we were indeed doing a good job. God didn't make them to be trophies for us to hold up to show the world how great we were doing. And He didn't make them to be in our image . . . only in His. We need to be careful not to tell them to resist bowing to the world's pressures at the same time we ourselves are bowing to the world's pressures. It's a thing.

The Good News

We can see our kids just as they are and celebrate the heck out of exactly who *they* are—no comparisons needed. As you may sometimes do, I can find myself scrolling through social media accounts of fellow parents. Around graduation I was doing just that to catch up on what my son's peers were doing next. As I noted moms and dads mentioning kids who had grand plans and who had received all the awards and accolades, I found myself weirdly thinking, *Wow, they must be really good parents*. And while I'm sure they are, the awards and accolades are not actually indicators of good parenting. Plenty of kids with good parents do not have honor cords or plans. And many moms and dads have gotten their kids through school despite the kids' anxiety, depression, and academic struggles (like at least one of mine). I can see in these parents' eyes the love they have for their kids. They, too, are really good parents.

I had to remind myself to celebrate wins. Personally, I got super excited when my boy—who finished high school architecture, construction, and design classes by the skin of his teeth after months of hard work that earned him frequent Cs—was awarded a fancy drill on honors night. The world needs more of this kind of celebration because those stories of *overcoming* might impress us all just as much as the kids who got accepted to Harvard.

And when the world doesn't see their gifts, it is really important that you do. You need to be their lead cheerleader if they struggle. Each of our children deserves to become exactly who God designed them to be, and we are here to support that.

What our kids need in this hard world is real-life relationships with us. They need us to cheer them on, just like we needed our parents to do the same. We may not be parenting ourselves, but we can re-create some of the slowness and magic of growing up before the world became more complicated. We can slow down and really see who they are and lean into the idea that there is a way to parent gently for relationship and connection.

Long Story Short

- We are raising our kids in an entirely different time and need to do things differently than our parents did, even if we loved our upbringing. And if we didn't love it, we *can* make a change!

- Learn about and acknowledge what your kids' lives are really like. Comments beginning with "back in the day" or "you should" don't help them move forward.

- Become an expert on what works for each of your children. There may be different strategies and rules for each human in your home.

- Celebrate your kids exactly as they are.

- Focus on how you can keep your kids connected to you and the family overall.

Dear Lord,

Remind me that I am not parenting myself, even when I want to be. I know my kid is different than I was. I know You have created each of us in Your image, but sometimes that is where the sameness seems to end. Help me get to know each of my people as their very own selves and to give them each what they need. Please help me remember we cannot go back to a simpler time, although maybe we can bring a simpleness to this one if we try.

Dear God, walk beside me as I celebrate this beautiful human You made and have trusted me with. Be with us both as we find all the many ways to be perfectly okay in Your world. You have created all this for us. When things are off the rails and I have no idea what to do, please help me take the next right step for the human in front of me.

Amen.

CHAPTER 6

Teens and Friendship

Say Goodbye to Planned Playdates and Hello to No Longer Being Able to Pick Their Friends

I watched her walk into the building and prayed today would be the day. *Please, dear God, let her find a friend. Let someone see how amazing she is and want to eat lunch with her. Do not let her sit alone. Also, could that friend You send be one who makes only good choices? Thank You. I trust You. Amen.*

I was desperate for my girl to find someone she could connect with outside of school. I had been agonizing over this first day of high school for weeks, knowing it would be so hard. And it was. She looked so little as she walked into the big brick building with her backpack on and her carefully picked first-day-of-school outfit that would hopefully both blend in and make her look cool. I knew she was trying to keep it together. So was I.

My hands gripped the steering wheel until my knuckles were white as I gave her an enormous "you can do this" smile when she looked back over her shoulder. Her expression said, *I'm okay, but also I'm terrified*, then she faced what was to come next: a sea of students, and not one was there waiting to see her.

As soon as she disappeared into the building, I slumped down in my seat and cried. I had been holding it all in, and it needed to come out right there in the drop-off line apparently. This was just like that first day of kindergarten, but my heart hurt in a new and different and deeper way for her. The stakes were way higher than when she was five. Now friends meant everything, and we couldn't fix it if her friendships were not working. I longed for the days when I could find a pal to come over and all would be well.

Her best friend from the year before had spread her wings to another group over the summer, slowly becoming "too busy" to hang out at our house or take trips to the mall. My girl had found herself unmoored, with no one to step into her childhood best friend's shoes, so she was not meeting a tried-and-true pal on that first day of high school. It suddenly no longer mattered that she and her best friend forever had held hands when walking into first grade. Or had had a million and one sleepovers. Or had planned on all the things they would do together in high school. It was made clear there had to be a parting of ways.

As an educator, I understood. I had seen it play out this way time and again. It was a normal part of kids growing up. The separation of friends was often the only way each of them could find who they really were. These were the years where all the changes in their brains drove them to try to fit in with their peers and move away from their parents. They were trying on different groups, leaving friends behind in the process without meaning to and without malice. The teacher in me got it.

As a mom, I was dying in my heart. Her people had to be in there somewhere, but would her bruised soul have the confidence to find them?

What We Can't Do

We cannot fix their friendship problems for them. The times when we could just hold their hands and walk them over to a new friend have sailed. They have to do this on their own, and we can't even call another mom to try to change things. That would not be helpful in any way at this stage in their lives; plus, it would be humiliating to them.

Instead, texts fly from kid to kid, and if a kid is not "in," they just have to *wait*. And if that text never comes? Misery. Absolute, pure misery. Watching our kids sit in loneliness is *hard*.

As a bonus, helping kids navigate friendships through middle and high school involves low-key reliving your every friendship nightmare, mixed with all-new ways kids can be cruel and exclusive. It's so hard not to feel in your heart the times when you were left out and lonely. You suddenly remember the name of the girl who didn't invite you to her sleepover, and you feel in your soul the pain of watching your friends all walk off together, sleeping bags in hand. And now, to save your child from the feelings you had, you may be tempted to go into full-battle mode.

What We Can Do

We can keep clear heads and solid perspectives and be the grown-ups. When you relive those hard moments, use them to help you know what might work to comfort your heartbroken kiddo. And don't be surprised when they have a variety of reactions as things get hard. They may fall into your lap sobbing.

They might need to be alone instead of sitting with you. They may take it all in stride while you are a hot mess. Just bring all that empathy, and remember how big these feelings are. They need you to stay solidly in the "you are going to be okay" camp when friendships go awry.

Hard as it is, we need to keep it chill so our kids don't feel any additional social pressure from us, because that is the last thing they need. An abundance of words can feel like a lecture to our teens, so listen a lot. Try not to ask too many questions, because that can feel like blame. They may read between our lines and wonder if we think they are not good enough too. So, get to the bottom of things with few words or questions and lots of listening. *Closed mouth, open ear holes.* No problem, right? You know by now this is not a skill set that comes easily to me. I pretty much like to share my every feeling, talk until I have no words left, and ask every question I can think of.

Luckily I had other tools to help guide both my kid and me through these rough waters. I leaned back into what I knew to be true about friendships and veered away from the many emotions I felt about the whole situation. Here are some things to remember when it gets tough:

- Expect changes in friend groups, and prepare for this. Normalize friends coming in and out of your kids' lives. They will need this skill for the rest of their days on this planet.

- Embrace whomever they are embracing if you can. You might not understand the appeal of certain friends, especially if those friends seem very different from the kind of kids you hung out with back in the day.

- We need to help them build strong inner compasses so they can trust their own guts when it comes to other people. This comes through having conversations and helping them reflect on people they meet and choices they make. I tell each of mine that God put that voice inside them for a reason and that they should listen to it.

- Help them know which humans can be trusted to be close to their hearts and which ones they may need to provide a little boundary for. Asking them how the friend makes them feel about themselves is helpful here.

- Do not get involved in the popularity game. It is all fake, and it doesn't matter in this life or the next. If you push your kids in this area, they will feel they are coming up short in your eyes. It doesn't matter where they fall in the false hierarchy of middle or high school. God loves them, and so do you, just as they are. They just need a buddy or two they can be with. That is enough.

If they are trying on different ways of acting to fit in to different friend groups, this, too, is totally normal. Just look down a middle school hallway. Even the kids who are trying to be different with crazy clothes and wildly dyed hair look the same as one another. You'll see packs of kids with the same "rebel" outfit walking next to packs of kids in the same sporty clothes, walking next to kids wearing jeans and flannel shirts. They distinguish themselves together. The drive can be strong. We need to step in only if our kids are miserable or off the rails with their behavior.

Whew. I think we have established that none of this is easy. But you've got this.

What Happened for Us

I wasn't prepared for the disruption to friendships that our kids can go through. The first time it happened, it threw us all for a loop. Eventually we were able to see this as a fresh start, although it took a while to find our footing.

When one of my people found herself in between friend groups, we talked a lot about the people she knew from clubs and classes and who from there might be a good fit as a friend. She then used every ounce of bravery in her soul to ask a classmate she thought seemed nice to hang out. It is not easy to put your heart on the line for friendship. It requires vulnerability and risk-taking. I was so proud of her.

As I drove the two girls to the coffee shop, I realized that starting new friendships can be just as hard as dating and that our kids need practice and guidance in forming new relationships during this formative time. The girls were silent and nervous in the back seat, so I (of course) tried to spark some awkward conversation, having wished I had coached my daughter in a few things they could talk about or some questions she could ask. But ultimately as a result of this one invitation for coffee, my girl was blessed with a friendship that lasted for a few solid years and was one of the strongest she had in her life at that point.

My son also started over with new friends after his tried-and-true group disbanded. He stayed in touch with some and found brand-new people too. Plus, he found friends through the online world, and these were trusted and valuable friendships for him. The whole "make new friends and keep the old" idea is actually good advice for our people.

They are not all going to be wins, though. The day may come when your child calls you from school, sobbing into her phone, able only to tell you she is sick and you need to come right away. When you probe a little further, you find out the bad belly she is calling about is really coming from a broken heart. Nothing quite prepares you for having your tall kiddo cry with her head in your lap after overhearing her friends talking about her on the stairway of the high school.

"They said I was a toxic person and horrible! And when they saw me, all they could say was, 'Well, this is awkward,' and then laughed. I know we haven't been getting along, but why would they do that?" She was crushed. And I felt crushed for her.

None of our kids are their best selves all the time. On this day, my girl's friends certainly weren't. Mean girls (and boys) seem to be such a time-honored tradition in our world that people have made both a play and a movie about them. Books have been written, and I'm pretty sure a song or poem or two have as well. And I *know* that doesn't make our kids feel a bit better—because when it happens to them, it feels like no one has ever felt this sad or betrayed or disappointed by a friend.

I get it. I remember finding a note passed between friends that was full of meanness, and it took me two solid minutes of rereading it to understand it was about me. I wanted to call my mom and get picked up from school too (and let's face it, I probably did).

On that day of my girl being heartsick, I drove her home. It felt like the right thing to do. Caring for her mental health when things got really low was like caring for her physical body had she gotten an injury in gym class. We tend to them in times of need. This was certainly a time of need.

I wished a simple Band-Aid or even a cast would fix her heartbreak. Instead, our medicine looked like stopping and getting Starbucks and heading for the couch. We watched a romcom, and I let her cry. She took social media off her phone so things wouldn't get worse (highly recommended anyway). We took it day by day, all of us in the family coming around her until she felt a bit better. We could not fix her pain, but we could sit by her in that pain—letting her feel it but also letting her know she was not alone. We could help her through this transition.

That is a really hard thing to do, isn't it?

You may have a kid who goes the other way—one who leans into the "mean group" and tries to fit in. When they find themselves in the middle of hard friend circles, we need to remember they may be driven pretty hard to be in a group. This is all part of the adolescent brain development and is perfectly normal, but it can also become unhealthy if left unchecked. We must be there to set boundaries when needed and to remind them who God made them to be.

There was a time that mean kid was me. I had my friend Jan come for a sleepover. The next morning, right after she left, I got a call from someone in the "in" group saying that Jan was now considered "out." I just went along with it. I didn't stick up for her or say we had a great time. Instead, I agreed with all the terrible things my friend on the phone was saying about her. Worse, I added to them. I pulled the phone under the table with me and really leaned into the whole thing, trying to secure my place in the group with my meanness.

I didn't realize my mom could hear me talking. You can imagine my surprise when she suddenly grabbed my feet, dragged me out from under the table, took the phone, hung it up, and just *looked* at me. I felt horrible and humiliated and had not a word to defend myself. I don't remember my mom's exact words, but I know they likely started with "Amy Rebecca Betters . . ." Whatever my mom said was very wise, because thirty-seven years later I still go back to this moment and remember how I felt about betraying my friend. I made a decision right then to be a different person. I'm pretty sure I was also grounded from the phone.

You might find yourself dragging your kid out from under the table by their ankles. All the grace for our people and for us. But we need to use these moments to teach our kids who they want to be. Our kids will be hurt, but they may also hurt people. We need to parent them through all of it.

The Good News

I really do believe we find our people eventually (although some of us are finding ourselves between friend groups as adults, right?), and for some kids this will just happen later in life. Not everyone makes their lifelong friends in middle or high school. We need to normalize this too. My sweet and wonderful middle girl—who tried and tried to find her people all through middle and high school with pockets of near success—finally found a wonderful group of friends who appreciate her for *her* (and whom she has a ton in common with) when she got to college. It has been a wonderful gift, and she appreciates these people. (So. Do. I.)

During this whole endeavor, we as a family had her back, and together we are stronger for it. It is the job of the family to fill in gaps when no friends are to be found. And family can include family of origin, extended family, neighborhood family, friends you call cousins, church family—any and all of it. There are beauty and blessings to be had, so think outside the school when it comes to your kids' friendships.

In the end we want for them the beauty of friendship. And honestly I love many of my children's friends like they were my own. When our kids love their friends, we need to try to see the amazing qualities in the kids they love. Encourage them to come over, feed them, and ask them about their lives. They are important to your kids, and that should mean they are important to you. These special friends fill our hearts and are amazing additions to our family.

You want to have the house with all the shoes in the hallway because the kids are there. (Or maybe you'd rather want to know the mom who loves that. Send your kid to that house with a bag of chips; then put your feet up, knowing your kid is in good hands.) It is all about helping our kids find community and then being a good human in that space.

Our kids deserve beautiful friendships. It is so worth our time and support to help them find at least one.

Long Story Short

- Give your kids space to try on different friendships. They may choose friends that are different from those you might have chosen for them. This is okay.

- Build your parent community so you know about your kids' friends. Talk to parents when you're at events and when you are milling around waiting for your kids. The connections you make are important too.

- Listen, listen, listen. And believe what they tell you. Ask few questions, and give advice when asked. But mostly, listen. Offer nonjudgmental advice and coaching.

- Shut out the social noise. Popularity is fake. Social media is only one side of anyone's life. It doesn't matter what your kids' friendships look like, only what they feel like.

- Don't make your worries their worries.

- Make your family a safe place to combat loneliness. Fill in the gaps when friendships are rough with those closest to you.

- Cherish their good friends. They are a gift.

Dear Lord,

Please watch over our kids and their friendships. Send them people who will understand their hearts and love them for who they are. Remind us to be open to the people they love. Let not crazy hair colors or weird piercings deter us from seeing the kid inside that wants to be friends with our kid. Help us discern what to say and what not to say to gently steer our people toward friends who are good for their hearts and away from those who are not.

Please hold our children close when they feel lonely, friendless, and awkward. Walk beside them in the hallway at school and at that darn lunch table. Send them just one friend they can really be themselves with. And if it happens that our kid is the mean kid, send us the words to help them start again. Help them be the good in the world. Be with them, Lord. And with us too.

Amen.

CHAPTER 7

Cellphones and Social Media

Everyone Has a Phone, and Everyone's Parents Leave Them Alone About It: Lies Your Teens Will Tell You

It was all one giant ball of conflict waiting to happen right from the start. I should have known what was coming by the way the child threw his backpack onto the table and then threw his body into the corner of the couch with a giant accusing sigh aimed in my direction.

"Mom. Seriously. I am the only one with a loser phone their parents locked down. The ONLY ONE. Every single one of my friends is on Snapchat. ALL OF THEM. And that is where they make plans, and I'm so left out, because if you are not in the group, you are forgotten. You are making me into a giant loser who cannot do anything. It's not fair!"

The child in question then glared at me as if I were indeed ruining his life. This look is now a default facial option, and I am not here for it.

I decided to go with logic and name a few people I knew whose parents monitored their phones and even more those I knew were not on Snapchat. My choice was questionable because logic affects exactly nothing in the teenager's brain.

"Okay, finnnnne. But I am *practically* the only one and will never have any friends at all, ever. Do you want me to just sit alone at home every single day?"

This did not actually sound bad to me in light of some of the things I knew were coming.

I calmly smiled and offered him a hug. Parenting level: expert.

"A hug? Really? No thank you!"

Eye roll. Stomping off. I was not liked at this moment, and I was okay with that. From the moment we even start negotiation around cellphones with our teenagers, we need to make our peace with not being liked.

Dear parent of newly minted teens, remember how your kids are liars? You need to remember this when talking to them about cellphones because they will also be fairly good liars about this issue.

They will tell you pretty much anything to get what they want, and what they want is *a phone.* With all the apps. They are desperate to fit in with the kids they see each day at middle school. Remember what we know about those brains. The power is real. They are going crazy about this, because in their minds, phones seem essential for fitting in. In some ways this might even be true.

What We Can't Do

We cannot turn back time; phones are here to stay. This is a giant, crazy topic that holds lots of feelings for everyone involved, so I just present to you my current best thinking based on what the world is throwing at us right now.

As we know, this world is overall a completely different place than it was when we were entering our teen years. Passing notes has turned into social media, which would blow our teenage minds, not to mention the minds of our parents.

We want to protect our kids. We do. But we must also prepare them to live in the world that is so big and crazy. How can we possibly know the best course of action? Give them all the things and try to help them? Give them none of the things and hope it all works out? Land somewhere in between?

No matter what, you will have to make the decision about when they will get a phone. The right time is dependent on the child. Some are ready sooner, some later. So you need to know your kid and what they can handle.

Then you will have to decide how to handle said phone. As an educator I have learned two things: (1) Social media is not made for developing brains, and (2) kids will be motivated to get to it no matter what you do.

In our house, I do not actively police any kids' phones once they have them. They know I can and will ask to see them if I am worried, but I know they are able to stay on top of all the ways to hide things. I keep all their passwords and codes just in case. Next is what I do instead of a regular phone check.

What We Can Do

We can hold our ground, hold off on jumping in, and then stay connected. First, we don't give them social media until their brains are a bit more developed and they are squarely in the high school years. If they don't have it, I don't have to check it, and this is just way easier. This is our current plan for our fifth and final pancake, so if I mess it up here, I do not get another chance. For us this lockdown includes no private viewing of YouTube or Google or any search engines at all during middle school. All searching on Google and watching videos on You-

Tube can be done in common spaces where it is easier to see what they are doing online.

This decision is backed up by research and the experiences of my older kids, who have lots of cautions for the younger ones. I'm going to listen to their voices. I think they have some wisdom. They recognize that what kids are dealing with now is already so different from what they did in middle school. They are so happy they didn't have the latest social media then. Each of our older kids has directly told us social media is a bad idea, and I believe them. They see way more than we do.

TikTok, Snapchat, and other popular apps can be hilarious and fun for those whose frontal lobes are ready to rock, but for our middle school and even high school kids they can be a dumpster fire. The algorithms will serve them content that is not necessary to their lives. They are not prepared to deal with the massive amounts of disinformation, super-sexualized situations, and bullying—which is a whole thing. So many of the bad things that have happened at the middle and high school level have their roots in social media. As an educator I wish none of our middle school kids had access.

As our youngest gets ready to embark on his journey as a first-time cellphone user, this is the one area where he has more rules than his siblings did at that age. For my high schoolers who currently have social media, I have suggested they delete it when I start to see it becoming a problem, but I also know their tricks. Kids will look up socials on a friend's phone, create fake accounts, and basically find work-arounds. I see a lot in my line of work, and kids talk. They are crafty.

In trying to find a solution here, so much of it goes back to connection. Instead of me grounding them and walking away, leaving them without tools to regulate their social media use when they get it back again, I help them listen to their own inner voices that might suggest they need to ground themselves from it. This is a great strategy to improve their mental health and teach them better long-term habits. So, when I observe too much scrolling, too much conflict, too much comparison, the discussion starts. They need to notice what it is doing to them and know when it is too much.

One of my kids is so good at this. Another needs to talk about how social media is making her feel, what she is seeing, etc. To me the sweet spot is watching kids reflect and knowing what they can handle. This builds the ongoing conversation we must have about social media.

The problem is that the teenage brain isn't always designed to know what it can handle, so teens might not know what is too much until it is too late. And that can be catastrophic. We have all heard the news stories about kids who have taken their own lives after online bullying and social media threats. Additionally, social media use can train teen brains to crave the rewards of numerous likes and views in a time when their brains are not ready to resist the temptations around this. It can actually change their brain chemistry and doesn't lead to our kids being their best selves. These types of social interactions can also leave them feeling lonelier instead of filled up like they would through real-life interaction with peers.[2] So we need to stay in the game and help them learn about their own limits. It is hard and worthy work.

We cannot become the world's ultimate snoop either, as tempting as that may be. While you can access their texts, social media, photos, contacts, and so many things, that doesn't mean you should. Can you imagine your parents being able to listen to every word you said to your friends when you were growing up? If they could have tracked your every movement, read every note you passed in school, and seen every word you wrote and photo you took anywhere, anytime?

That thought might make you squirm. Who would have wanted their parents to see everything? Our kids feel the same way. So, while we have a lot of access to information about our children, that doesn't mean we should be looking at all of it. Do our teenagers deserve privacy? As separate humans, they sure do. And if we are going to have lifelong relationships with them, we have to honor their privacy. We need to guide them while letting them have some things that are just theirs.

The truth is we no longer can know all the things. Our kids are moving away from us to become their own selves, *which is exactly what they are designed to do.* So not only do we have to teach them, but we also must trust them. Trusting a teenager can be a tricky business, especially when they have given us reason not to.

Do not be surprised if your teenager does something dumb with their phone, like sending mean texts, downloading something inappropriate, or whatever. They will mess up. We have to give them a way to rebuild it after they do break our trust. In our family we call this working with the Bank of Trust. Make too many withdrawals from your account and you have no trust left. With no trust, you may not even have a phone to worry about. The only way forward is to make some deposits. So we create opportunities for those deposits. We do not want our kids' mistakes to end up becoming their identity. We want them to see themselves as capable and strong and to see us as people who are on their side and who will both protect and guide them in a reasonable manner.

Communication is key. We need to let them know that if they go off the rails, we are here to help them course correct and that they should never be afraid to tell us they have messed up. If they are in a scary situation, we don't want to be the ones making it scarier. We want to be the ones who help them find a solution, not nail them to the wall for making a mistake, even if it is a big one. The more we can trust them to trust themselves and to talk to us when they are uncertain, the more they will come to us.

What Happened for Us

We were sitting around the table one night during dinner after my bigs were home from school.

"Ugh," one of them said, "I need to block another one."

"Another what?" I asked.

"Another kid from my high school. Why on earth do these guys think it's a good idea to just send people nudes?"

I almost dropped the macaroni.

"Umm . . . people just send you nude pictures for no reason?"

The other girl chimed in. "They sure do. It's disgusting," she said, grabbing her plate and helping herself to some salad like we were talking about the weather.

I stopped the meal, and we *talked*, because these kids thought this was normal. For them it *was* normal: You see it, you block it, and you have some macaroni. But it is not any kind of normal we want for our kids. The kids doing this? They were athletes, good students, kids from "nice families," you name it.

I have friends who have found their kids engaging in so much weirdness on the internet—reposting content they shouldn't, sharing details of their lives that shouldn't be open for public consumption. We have learned that if we are not following their socials, then trusted aunts, uncles, cousins, and friends need to be. If you are worried, you can take a peek at their phone. This is why you have their codes and passwords for an emergency, when you really think they are in the weeds. But also remember, if you find nothing, they may be hiding things where you cannot see them. Talk to them early and often.

We have to keep our voices at the table with them. We must know what is out there and ask them the hard questions about what they are seeing and doing online. Bring it into the light. Assure them there is no shame if they mess up, if they send or receive a picture that is questionable, or if they stumbled on something and now can't stop thinking about it. We want them to talk to us about all of it. *All* of it.

The Good News

If we are connected to our teens, we have the best chance of getting a little bit of our wisdom into their ears about this topic. We need to walk alongside them to help them through mistakes they make and to help keep them from becoming addicted to technology, even innocently. My kids are sick of my sharing statistics and stories of things I have read online, and they are surprised when I know about new things happening on social media, new apps that are out there, and what is happening with technology. It's a lot of work to stay in the loop because the loop is always changing.

There is even a trend where some of our kids are seeking less sharing and scrolling and more living. Some are asking for flip phones instead of smartphones, finding ways to monitor and hold themselves accountable for the amount of time they spend on social media. They recognize the danger and are instead using technology for good connections and learning. It isn't all bad, and the more we know, the better off we all will be. No hiding out allowed on this one, friend. We need to be a part of this world. Our kids might even have to lead us.

Long Story Short

- Our kids' brains are wired right now to try to be just like everyone else. This is why they ask for and want whatever their friends have. It meets their need to fit in.

- It is okay not to let them have all the things. Make intentional decisions about phones and social media use. Listen to them, even if they sound crazy, because they need to feel heard and need a say in the family system.

- Remember to focus on boundaries and relationships. Both are things our kids need to learn to handle in their own lives as well.

- They will thank you someday for helping them navigate this time. Try to remember this when they tell you they hate you. (They don't.)

- Don't make a regular practice of checking everything on your teen's phone, or they will find ways to hide it. Instead, always keep communication open.

- Stay up to date on the latest technology and apps kids use. We have to know what is going on so we can have knowledgeable conversations with them.

Dear Lord,

Please let us use Your gift of technology for good and help our teens do the same. Thank You for my really fun virtual Hay Day farm, and please ban TikTok with some sort of godly curse—at least all the dumb and inaccurate and terrifying parts. I'm fine with keeping the funny videos and the ones of babies and cats.

Please help our kids listen to the voice You have planted in their hearts so they stay away from everything the world is shouting at them through their phones. Give them the strength to set their phones down, and please help us stay one step ahead of the things that will cause them harm. Let them use their powers of problem solving for good and not for keeping scary things from us. Please remind them to text us back and to call us when they need to.

Let their social media presence be life-giving and nothing they are humiliated by when they are in their thirties. And keep them from the worst parts of social media bullying. Please, God, keep them from sending and receiving nudes. And help us be good examples to them with our own technology use.

Amen.

House Rules and Chores

How to Get Your Kids to Do Stuff They Need to Do Without Driving You Crazy

Our household has a nightly ritual that I call the ceremonial fighting over the cleaning of the kitchen. My kids have been in charge of cleaning the kitchen after dinner since they could stand on a stool and help wash the dishes. Yet, somehow, it still seems to be a giant surprise to them that they have to clean the kitchen. *Oh my goodness, what do you mean there are dirty dishes? And a gross pan? And we have to wipe down the counters too? What is this nightly madness? How can this be happening* again *when it just happened twenty-four hours ago?*

I feel the same way about making dinner, so I get it.

Once they get over the shock, they start dividing the labor. This takes roughly a thousand years and the tactical skill of an army general. They will divide jobs down to how many square inches of the kitchen counter each person has to wipe. The person who washes the pan may be different from the person who washes the five dishes that didn't fit in the dishwasher. (Apparently, in teenager kitchen-cleaning math, one dirty pan equals five regular dishes.) There is an entire list of unwritten rules that they all abide by. Loudly. And with great debate. And above all it must be *fair*. So. Fair.

But you know what isn't fair? The fact we parents have to listen to all of this ensue. They could legit be done cleaning the kitchen in the time it takes them to plan cleaning the kitchen. Each one of my children seems to be covered in a chore-resistant coating, because any job we give them slides right off and they can't seem to pick it back up and grasp it.

Many times I have thought my kids were flat-out trying to either kill us with their kitchen arguing or get us to abandon the whole idea of making them do it. It almost works. I often want to go running into the kitchen screaming, "Never mind! I will do it! Just go away so I do not have to listen to this tom-foolery for another minute!"

But we stick it out every time. The only way *to* our destination is *through*, and that means we let our kids clear the kitchen for thirty hours when it would take us fourteen minutes. Let's hope they are learning something. Anything. Preferably something about the value of helping and living in community and taking personal responsibility. Or even just that Mom and Dad do not back down when it comes to chores.

What We Can't Do

We cannot expect our kids to understand the need to do things like chores. The need for general maintenance of their lives, their rooms, and our home does not seem to come naturally to their teenage brains, so we need to show them the connection. Telling them to "just do it" doesn't work. You will feel like you are talking to a wall.

They need to see the *why* of things like laundry and vacuuming and putting away groceries because it apparently is not obvious to them. They have told me to my face that they do not care whether the house or their clothes are clean. They think they have better things to do with their time. But we want our kids to realize that our family is a team, just like God's family on earth is a team and that we all have a responsibility to work within it using our gifts for the good.

I've tried all the things that don't work, like nagging, reminding, and begging. I've tried yelling about putting away their backpacks, their shoes, and their things in the kitchen. I've lectured about hoarding dishes and silverware in their rooms and then plopping them on the counter as if some magic fairy were going to scrape weeks of crust and grime off them so they would magically be clean when we needed them next.

One day I lost it a little and went into flat-out teacher mode. I grabbed some poster board and wrote out every single job it took to keep our house running: cleaning toilets, mowing the lawn, paying the bills, pairing the socks, putting away dishes, weeding the flower beds, feeding the cats, scooping the litter, changing sheets, making sure we had groceries . . . all of it. It all went on these posters. I taped these on the sliding glass doors in our family room, and the kids were stunned at how many things we had to do around the house.

Next, I asked them to tell me who was currently responsible for doing these jobs. I have not heard them say *mom* so many times since they were two. They owned a few jobs like cleaning the kitchen and mowing the lawn, but it became really clear they expected me or their dad to do the bulk of the work. Mom paid the bills; Dad took out the garbage; Mom or Dad did the laundry; Mom did the vacuuming and the dusting.

At this point, our house was in a bit of shambles. While these jobs were mine at the time, I worked almost full-time and so was not pulling them off in the least. I asked the kids to go around the house and notice whether our current system was working. Were all these jobs done? One glance in our toilets and the answer was pretty obvious.

They looked around, and Sam said, "I don't want to be mean, but you are not doing a very good job."

I said, "You're right. My job is impossible. There is no way I can do all these jobs and do them well. So, what are we going to do?"

One of them said smartly, "Okay, we *get it*, Mom. We need to do more of these jobs. We will do better."

And then the angels sang, and from that moment on, my kids always cleaned their rooms and did their jobs without complaining and my house always looks amazing.

Not. Even. Close.

What We Can Do

We can help our kids understand what it means to be in a family living in community. So, honestly, first we must decide that we will let some things go. You will find zero perfectly clean bedrooms in my house, for example. We are realistic in our expectations.

But for the things that matter, we have had to circle back a million and one times. There have been hard times in the form of something called consequences. So we make a plan with our kids based on one question: *What should happen if you don't do your part?* Then we keep them accountable to that thing.

Life has a way of teaching all the lessons. We can't be afraid to let kids learn. We have to allow them to feel the consequences of their actions and not rescue them from a hard thing they created.

The consequences we set are just boundaries around what happens when kids are not doing their part. It can look something like this:

If the kitchen isn't clean, no one is leaving on a date with their significant other—even if you told them you were leaving now or you really want to see them. If you have tickets to something fun or there is some sort of timely thing going on, then we understand as long as you let the family know or you ask a sibling to fill in for you. Also the fact that you all have to poop immediately upon the kitchen needing to be cleaned is some sort of phenomenon that we really need to take up with the doctor.

These are all words I think I have said to my people. They have missed out on things because they needed to do their stuff first. It's a thing. And they learn from this. Just last week, my son got up at six o'clock on a Sunday morning to do his jobs (clean the basement and his bathroom) so he could go on a breakfast date with his girlfriend. If you heard the angels sing one Sunday morning, this is why.

Lest you think we have it all figured out, on this same day, another kid played on her phone all the livelong day and when she wanted to leave was told she was going nowhere.

What Happened for Us

I would say every one of my kids gets the whole "we live in community so we all help out" thing now. They understand with their hearts probably 98 percent of the time. They show us with their actions about 63 percent of the time, but they are always getting better. This number can fluctuate, however.

Full disclosure: I just got done sobbing in the corner of my couch because my offspring currently seem 110 percent uninterested in helping with anything. They very nicely agree to do things, but our follow-through today is more like 13 percent. I'm exhausted from being the force that drives everything—taking stock of the jobs to be done, reminding them, asking them to get off their phones, and answering endless "Mom, do you know where my" questions. I'm discouraged and sad. There are seasons when our parenting doesn't seem to be bearing any fruit. We swear we have planted all the right seeds, but nothing is showing up. Those moments can kick us low. I'm currently fantasizing about living alone in a small cottage, leaving the kids with Todd and wishing him luck. Maybe I'll take my cats, minus the one who keeps peeing in my front room.

I'm also honestly thrilled and excited about having all these humans in my home, even when the mess comes with them. Our hearts have room for both extremes of feelings. We can be happy about our progress one minute and want to hide somewhere to sob about how hard it is the next. Cry when you need to, and keep watering those seeds. I swear something wonderful will grow in its own season.

So we just keep on reinforcing the need to work together, and we help them learn to weigh out how much time they have and how long tasks should take. We need to teach and guide them into helping out and not become frustrated when their efforts look like they haven't tried at all.

In our house we do have a few people with ADD/ADHD, which is a whole book in itself. If you have neurodiverse kids, you may need additional strategies to help them navigate getting things done at home and in the world. Here are a few of ours (which work for kids who are not neurodiverse as well):

- See the good in what they have done, and name it for them, even if it's an attempt.

- Help them build a sense of time by using countdown clocks or having them monitor time with alarms.

- Teach them to break tasks into small chunks.

- Help them learn how they can fill up their emotional and physical energy tanks if doing tasks like chores depletes them.

- Offer small rewards to accomplish large goals.

The Good News

When I am super overwhelmed by trying to get my kids to work with me around the house, I go back *again* to relationship and connection. How can we show them that God created us to work together in our home and world for the good of everyone?

We stop and talk with them regularly, because as our kids get older, they will work with us like roommates so they can learn to be good ones in the future. When they go to their own spaces and come back to ours, they will recognize how nice it is to have other people around to help clean the kitchen. By learning from consequences, they will become more responsible and do things like get up on time for their jobs all on their own—even though you were certain this would never be a thing for them.

It can all feel like a miracle. . . . You will occasionally come home to a clean kitchen and folded laundry when you didn't even ask anyone to do anything. While this is rare, it becomes more common as they grow. You will see those little seeds you watered start to sprout. Our hard work is worth it, friend. I promise.

Long Story Short

- Be a team. Include kids in the plan for any work that must be done in the house and rules that need to be made. Try to let them have a voice wherever possible.

- Empower them with the skills. Do not assume they know what it means to "clean the bathroom," for example, without giving them the specifics. Breaking down a task works better than yelling.

- Remind them that you are human and that you cannot do all the chores alone. Let them own the work that needs to be done as community members, not as helpers.
- Allow for natural consequences. If they break an agreement with you, there may be some discomfort to their personal schedule. Stay strong, and let them feel this.
- Writing things down is always helpful. Use Post-its to make lists of what needs to be done.

Dear God,

Please remind me these kids You have given me will not live in their own filth forever—or if they do, it won't always be in a room in my home. Please help me overlook their messy beds and the laundry that never leaves their baskets. Help me focus on the good in each of them and not on what is under their beds. Remove the scales from their eyes, and let them behold the dirt. Also remind me that my own room growing up was pretty much a pigsty, yet now I am a person who dusts light fixtures and wipes down baseboards (at least before big holidays). Nudge them to return their dishes to the kitchen before they mold, and help them see the spoon stuck in the napkin on the plate they are bringing back so that spoon doesn't meet its demise in the garbage can. Also remind me to buy more spoons since they are all almost gone again.

And, God, if they sleep through their alarm, maybe You could startle them awake with a little zap of adrenaline? They could use the push in the morning. And please help them find the value of hard work and let them practice that work on their really disgusting toilets.

Amen.

CHAPTER 9

Teenagers and Fashion

A Corset and Sunglasses Are Not an Outfit: When You're No Longer in Control

I was walking through the mall with my mom and daughters on a quest to find the girls outfits for the Christmas Eve church service. Of course, because we are us, it was December 23, so we had just this one day. No internet order to fall back on. We had been to roughly a bazillion stores to find something that was similar to what they had picked out on Pinterest or TikTok or some such nonsense. Each child had very specific requests, and frankly, none of it was what I would have chosen for them to wear.

The girls were sauntering in front of my mom and me, their long hair still drying from the snow because there was also a near blizzard outside. (Of course there was.) The girls were holding up their phones, showing each other the "outfit inspirations" they were going for. We walked toward one of the stores that the girls liked, which played music much too loud and contained too many shirts that were much too skimpy.

I am clearly not young.

My mom and I held up this or that for the girls, asking "What about this one?" and were met with a polite "maaaaaybe" or little shake of the head each time. After ten minutes it was clear we were striking out yet again. On top of it, everyone was getting hungry and tired.

As we walked to get coffee for the kid who "couldn't take another step" without one, I lamented to my mom, "How much do you miss Gymboree? Like I would give a million dollars to walk them in there and find them cute dresses while they watched cartoons in the back of the store, knowing they would just wear whatever we picked out as long as they could twirl in it."

What We Can't Do

We can no longer pick out all our kids' clothes. You will see something super cute at Target and will be tempted to bring it home, but you would be wasting your time and money. They will not wear it. They will not like it, either, because it is uncool for some reason or simply because you were the one to pick it out.

You need to face this fact immediately or spend years parting with your cash for a pile of clothes that will sit in closets and then head to Goodwill with price tags still on. I may or may not have done this and taken way too long to learn my lesson.

Going to the mall with this gang was something we had been doing since they were small. My mom always helped pick out matching Christmas dresses for all the granddaughters and ties and cute sweaters for the grandsons. They would all wear these without question or fail. But this was no longer the case.

The boys this year had been easy. I ordered what I wanted them to wear to church, and it arrived at our home. I bribed them with food to try it on, it fit, and they took it off and threw it on the floor. I made them pick it up and fold it, and it sat folded until it was time to wear it. The end.

The girls? Not so much.

There were the aforementioned TikTok videos, Pinterest boards, and Depop searches to factor in. There was their crusade against fast fashion to consider and the ethics of different stores to discuss. There was a quest for a turtleneck that someone wore on Instagram but was nowhere to be found in stores. And now we were apparently doomed to have nothing to wear, world without end, amen.

They now have their own ideas about fashion. They buy mom jeans and old-man sweaters from the nineties. And they look at me in my little Loft cardigans and tell me I "look good for a mom"—even though they sometimes wear my clothes. Trying to figure that out makes my head hurt.

On top of this, they do things like buy thrifted T-shirts with weird sayings on them, either cut them up so they are half shirts or make them into skirts, and then steal my old cardigans and their dad's largest hoodies to put over them.

Not all kids are thrifters or play the ethics card with different stores. I hear from some parents that their kids are fantastic mall shoppers but will wear only this or that brand. Many girls are purchasing leggings with little pockets (where they keep their phones, I guess) and wearing them as pants, which is a whole thing. These little tubes of leg fabric cost roughly a bazillion dollars, so if you can't win one way, I guess you lose in another.

They have their own specific ideas about what they want to wear, and their choices are endless. Just like we did at their age, they want to wear what they want and pretend they invented it.

What We Can Do

We can look for the beauty. Here is the thing: Our kids are flat-out beautiful despite the fact they take no advice from us or put no stock in our vision for their wardrobes.

Their pierced noses, dyed hair (which is no actual color that would grow out of a human head), and their clunky shoes . . . It's all so beautiful because *they feel* so darn beautiful. I love the thrifted jeans and the grandma sweatshirts and the fact they get so into thrifting because they are trying to help save our planet. The ones walking in the uniform of the moment—leggings, tennies, and the perfect branded long shirt—feel amazing, and it shows. I love it all.

I may not get a say, and they may think I look "good for a mom," but my soul is secretly here for all of this.

Under the umbrella of fashion, we need to address the important topic of body image. The number of messages teens get about their bodies online is insane. We need to make sure we are not adding to that noise and instead are combating it. I have learned we need to refrain from commenting on bodies. We don't need to talk about the shape or size of our kids—or anyone else. They don't need us to tell them when they are getting bigger or smaller. We need to be the ones reminding them they are as God made them and they are beautiful. When we are looking at clothes in dressing rooms, we can ask whether the outfit feels like it fits, how comfortable it is, and whether they feel great in it. That is all we need to say. Not "That looks too tight" or "It doesn't flatter your figure."

I have learned to appreciate the amazingness that is their self-expression. It is the persona they are trying on at the moment. It is nothing to be afraid of. They will not necessarily look like us or wear that thing we think will look great, but their clothing is like a window into their sweet souls. And they have figured out how to not only hide under hoodies as needed but also full-on walk the runway into school with a thrifted pair of boots and a Harley T-shirt. They are my heroes as I watch them from within my uniform of joggers and a cardigan, which I now wear day in and day out because the persona I am trying on is that of an old, comfortable lady. And it fits.

I can bite my tongue because I am reminded of the six-year-old who wore nothing but princess costumes for a year, the eight-year-old who wore his Spider-Man Halloween costume like it was a fashion choice, and the ten-year-old who wore a bandana tied around her hair like a little old lady every day. I can remember loving every bit of every phase, and I realize I've been practicing radical acceptance of everything about my people for many years now.

I can bite my tongue because these are not my choices to make. I release these choices to the ones who own them—my beautiful people, whose hearts and minds I care about way more than their fashion preferences.

I can bite my tongue because the ability to self-express through their bodies is something this generation is here for. And putting the focus on how they appear to the rest of the world is not a healthy approach to these beautiful bodies God has given them that He wants us to love. He sent Jesus to live in a physical body, to experience some of what we experience. And each and every body is made in God's own image. Look around and just thinking about that. Wow. If that doesn't make our bodies holy, I do not know what does.

Our bodies are holy in a bikini or in a snowsuit. They are holy whether our hair is dyed green or all the colors of the rainbow. All of it is from God. God made our bodies, and we need to embrace and love however our kids love their bodies so we do not override His voice inside them.

Even when they are begging for purple hair that I know isn't going to end well. Even when they are attempting to find the perfect thing they saw online that I am quite certain doesn't exist in real life. Even when their clothing choices look exactly the opposite of what I would choose for them.

I love it. I love them. I love seeing their vision of themselves in the world.

What Happened for Us

When it comes to church clothes, I have given up on anything fancy for my kids. I just want them to be clean and respectful in their dress, maybe like when they go to a nice restaurant. I still feel weird wearing jeans in church, so I usually dial it up a notch myself—although in most churches you will see people in jeans and even jerseys sporting their favorite football teams. On a recent Sunday at church, I looked down the row at my people. My boys were in their hoodie-and-sweatpants uniforms, and the girls were in a glorious array of sweatpants, flare pants, cardigans, man shirts, and weird T-shirts with giant emblems on them—basically a beautiful mix of thrift-shop finds and brand-name mall clothes. It would make zero sense to the untrained eye, but it was their way of "dressing up" for church.

It just so happened on this particular Sunday that the pastor read part of the poem "Warning," written by Jenny Joseph in 1961. It starts like this:

When I am an old woman I shall wear purple
With a red hat which doesn't go, and doesn't suit me.[3]

My mom has always loved this poem, and in turn I loved it too. My mom was on one side of me and my girls on the other when the pastor read this. Instantly, Lily tapped me on the shoulder and whispered, "Mom, I think I am already doing that!"

I looked at her and tears sprang to my eyes. "You sure are,

my beautiful girl." As I looked down at her sisters, I knew they were right there with her too.

These kids get it. They are living their best lives already in a way we might not have, and their fashion is a reflection of their wild hearts.

The Good News

They are finding themselves. They have no interest in being bound by what we think is cute or appropriate, yet it can be so hard to break out of the voices in our own heads that remind us modesty is everything. We now know that reinforcing modesty can also reinforce shame. This is the last thing we want. Instead, we need to keep telling these humans that they are as God made them exactly on purpose since the day they were born. Out of respect for the dear elderly neighbor across the street who doesn't see things the same way, they may need to rethink wearing that skimpy bikini when mowing the lawn, and they need to know what to wear in a more formal situation (time to lose the hoodies, boys) and how that is different than what they wear when hanging out with friends. But beyond that, their fashion should be their own way to express themselves.

I can tell my people honestly that they look beautiful. Their hearts are shining out through their faces and fashion, and they are great kids. Plus, a little belly button here or there never hurt anyone. Although I will always keep trying to find a shirt to cover mine.

Long Story Short

- Their fashion reflects who they are becoming. Be supportive if you can, neutral if you can't.

- Let their hair be their hair.

- Do not comment on their bodies, ever. Focus on comfort and how they feel in what they are wearing.

- Reinforcing modesty can also reinforce shame. Instead, talk about what is appropriate for different situations (church, school, parties, etc.).

- Don't be afraid to find joy alongside them as they experiment with their fashion!

Dear Lord,

Please bless the fashion choices of these children. Know that when they are in church wearing that thrifted shirt and crazy pants, they are still here to worship You and they mean no disrespect. I think You get it because You see their hearts. You know they are trying to match their outsides to their insides and their insides are going through puberty (which You designed), so that matching process can be a bit of a mess.

Help us love them well when they have the color hair You gave them and also when they dye it green, because You also gave them the gift of creativity. Above all, help them know they are fearfully and wonderfully made— and remind me of that too.

Amen.

CHAPTER 10

Teens and Dating

Teenage Love Is a Strong Force, and He'd
Better Not Honk from the Driveway

My son's first girlfriend was someone he hadn't yet met in real life. She didn't even live in the same town, and they learned about each other through social media and then by playing online games together. I had no idea he was even chatting with this girl until he had decided to meet her in real life. He basically ran out the door saying, "I have a date! The girls will tell you about it."

I was aghast, and every one of my kids looked at me like I was *crazy*.

"This is how we do it now, Mom. People meet this way all the time."

He had planned an exit strategy with his sisters in case this girl wasn't who she said she was. I was brought in the loop at the last moment. All I wanted was some intel about this girl, and I could find just a little after I resorted to using the only tool at my disposal: social media. I could at least see her public-facing page.

Falling in like and love will do crazy things to our teenagers, friend. *Crazy* things. Things that are even crazier than having a girlfriend you have never met. Then, once they meet, things quickly get real. And the trick is for us to somehow stay sane. By the way, don't say "Not my kid," because I promise you every one of your kids will do something you never saw coming.

What We Can't Do

We cannot ignore the new world of teenage dating that is vastly different than ours was. Back in the day, my parents had about a 99 percent chance of knowing the family of anyone I dated. We were all connected in many ways, even when I dated a boy who lived an hour and a half away. I met him at a Youth Encounter event, so my parents met his family, and they had some peace of mind when they found out that a friend of a friend knew the family well. (Also, I was the kid picking up boys at religious retreats, so another point for me.)

We are preparing our kids for a dating world we wouldn't have dreamed of when we were their age. If you were raised in the era of corded phones and notes being passed in the hallway, you know things were pretty contained. My parents often overheard my conversations with friends over the phone even though I stretched it into the bathroom to try to get a little privacy. My mom found notes in my pockets when she did the laundry and probably got a little info that way.

If someone wanted to ask me on a date, they had to call me on the phone or walk up to me and talk to me in real life. I guess they could have also passed a note with a "Check yes or no" or had a friend ask in their stead, but that is probably as removed as it got.

Things have *changed*. Kids are continually meeting other kids online—on dating and social apps. Their relationships are online, with rules we don't know or understand regarding what they are supposed to post and not post about the person they are in a relationship with. And here is a biggie: The idea of waiting for marriage to have a sexual relationship is considered way beyond old-fashioned.

To add yet another layer, kids are now open about identifying as gay or bisexual or any of the other parts of the LGBTQ+ rainbow. Having discussions with our kids is healthy and good, and I am here for it, knowing that this all can be hard on families and on kids because it often means the world won't treat them well. The strong opinions and heartfelt beliefs around this topic hold the potential to strain relationships with friends and extended family. We have chosen to lead with love in our family, leaning hard into the idea that we are all who God made us. We need to stay open and want our kids to always know they are loved by God and by us, right in the midst of their wrestling with the messy and sometimes uncomfortable realities around every aspect of their journey toward becoming the people He created them to be.

Because of this new world we all live in, parents need a new set of rules for thinking about relationships, and we have to involve our kids in this process. When kids say we don't get it, they are most often correct, so we need to stay curious. Some questions you can ask include these:

- How do things work in your reality when it comes to dating?

- Are people in your social circle dating?

- How are you finding people to date?

- How long do you feel you should know someone before you become exclusive?

- How often do you see the person you are dating, and how often should you still see your friends?

- What rules should we set around your being alone with your date? Around driving? Around driving the minivan?

Answers to these questions have varied for each of our kids as well as for each of their relationships. Because it is all so complicated, we need to sit down and talk with our kids about it all.

I'm pretty sure, in my day, my parents had to set a time for curfew, a rule about no boys in the bedrooms, and a rule about no talking on the phone after midnight. And he'd better not honk from the driveway. It didn't get much more complicated than that. Oh, how the world has changed.

What We Can Do

We can keep on being there, right in our kids' reality. Even if we wholeheartedly want our kids to wait to have sex until they find a spouse, statistics tell us most kids are not doing this. If we pretend this is untrue, it will still be true. Ignoring it will not make it go away. Therefore, we need to talk to our teens about dating and sex often.

Those of us who grew up in a purity culture need to understand that the things we were taught are not going to cut it for this generation. Simply telling today's kids "Wait for marriage, abstinence is the answer, and now we are done talking about it" will backfire. Frankly, purity culture created a lot of mystery, hurt, and shame around sex that leaked into our married years. We need to have very honest conversations about God's plan for sex in relationships—that God has designed sex for good and for bonding us together and for making wonderful babies and families. At the same time, we must be prepared to communicate what they need to know if they choose to have sex before we want them to. Pray for the best, and prepare for the worst. I know that may be very hard to hear and even harder to accept.

We need kids to understand more than just the surface reasons to wait. We need them to know why it is important to be very careful with their bodies and with their hearts. If our kids trust the wrong people with their bodies, there are potentially even bigger consequences than we ever had. Because of technology, anything they may send or receive that is a part of their sex life can be shared on social media at any time because digital communication can last forever.

Try as we might, the reality is we cannot always compete with the draw of the world or kids' biology. So our job is to help them be prepared for the consequences of whatever decision they make. We have a responsibility to educate them about birth control and heart control.

We need to help them understand that a breakup after a sexual relationship is more heartbreaking than after one without and that a pregnancy while still in high school will change the trajectory of their lives. It is important to have these conversations early—before they begin dating and before defenses are up. When that door is open, they are listening and they do trust us, especially if we stay connected and open to their thoughts and questions. Listen. Be truthful. Pray with them and over them. Take sex out of the darkness and into the light. It is hard, but they need us. The world is telling them so many things, so let us not be silent.

I have friends who have gone through pregnancy scares with both their daughters and their sons. If you find yourself in this situation with your kid, you want to be right there so you can put your arms around them when they are scared and worried. You want to remind them you love them and God loves them. They will need your guidance, and you do not want them handling it on their own. Teenagers can make dumb decisions they think are fine until they realize they aren't. And then those dumb decisions compound as they try to fix the first ones. They need us for the big things, so we need to make sure that door is open.

You will need to set aside your own feelings and fears so you can really listen and help them take the next right steps with their bodies, hearts, and souls. Then you can let our dear Lord above wrap His arms around you, love you, and help you take the next right steps as you guide this baby you love through some of the toughest moments imaginable.

This can be one of the hardest topics for parents to talk about. I get it. But start that conversation if you haven't. Ask your kids about what they see others doing. Ask them about themselves. And be ready to hear what they have to say, even if it is hard. Remember they need you, even when they think they can handle it all on their own. It is never too late to talk with them openly and honestly.

Bonus: What We Can Do to Help Our Kids Date Well

Just like in the good old days, kids' hearts can be flat-out broken, and there is not a darn thing we can do about it. You may be relieved. You may have seen this coming. You may wish they had not broken up with whoever it was. And every single feeling you've ever had when your own heart was broken may come up. You may want to teach and lecture and tell them it is all going to be okay.

We might be tempted to think about our kids' broken hearts in relation to our healed ones. While the gift of time has shown us how our broken hearts have healed, we know our kids' hearts will too, but they do not have this gift. We have gone on to fulfill many of our dreams and even have children. Our kids don't know whether any of these things will ever happen for them, though. So their broken hearts can come with a side of "Will I ever love again?" and "I'm going to be alone forever" or even "I am unlovable." But in this moment, you need to flat-out tell them it stinks and it's horrible and they don't deserve any of it. Coach them around what a relationship should be, while acknowledging their pain. We need to have all the empathy we can for their broken hearts. Remember how your own heart felt in that moment.

Remind them they are just fine on their own. Our kids need to see themselves as whole while not being part of a couple. For some kids this is easy. For others it can start to get tricky, and they will need some coaching here.

I was sitting with my older girls, and they were talking about someone a few years younger who they felt should break up with her boyfriend. They saw some red flags and thought the relationship should be done. One of them said, "I don't know why she doesn't just break up with him. I mean, it is not a healthy relationship, and she deserves more."

I looked at this girl and said, "Well, how well did that work when you were dating Peter?" And we laughed and laughed— because it hadn't worked at all. Each person has to work it out in their own time. We can see things they can't, and often all we can do is be there. We can say our piece when it needs to be said and then pray they listen. We must also be sure they are in a healthy place even while they are sad. And we must be ready to respond if we see them entering into depression over a longer period of time.

When our kids began dating, I made a few rules—oddly, they were rules *for me* around *their* dating. First, I would try to see the good in whomever they brought before us. As my kids have gotten older and are dating more seriously, this rule has become really important. I want to lead with love and connection and focus on what my kid loves about the person. After all, just like you can't pick their friends, you cannot pick the person they date.

Second, I vowed to encourage each of our kids to really think about what they want in a dating relationship and eventually a life partner. We can have conversations that make our kids think and see things a different way without telling them what to think. I want my kids to know the importance of being friends with whomever they are dating. I also want them to trust themselves when it comes to connecting with their partners, to know their worth in the eyes of God, and to keep what they value at the forefront.

If your kid brings home a love interest whom they see as so amazing but you see as a giant red flag shaped like a human person, it is not easy. Despite how right you are, your feelings about the red-flag human will not be heard if you say them out loud to your child. They will start to hide said red flag from you. Stay cool here, my friend.

When your child starts dating, here are some ideas to get the conversation rolling in an easy and neutral way, even if you are just trying to get to know the person they are smitten with. These questions and lead-ins will help your teen reflect on the relationship, as well as help you get to know what they are thinking:

- Tell me what you love about them.

- Tell me what they love about you.

- What do you think makes you compatible?

- What do they like to do for fun?

- Tell me about their family.

- How do they make you feel?

- I can see you are upset after talking to Bobby. That happens a lot. Are you okay?

- You deserve to be with a person who lifts you up. How does Alice do that in your relationship?

These can help you open up a good talk and get some of your teen's perspective. The last two questions are a little more loaded and can be used if you are starting to see things that are a little off in their relationship.

If you are concerned about your kid's significant other but really want to keep the lines of communication open, here are some things you will want to say but *shouldn't*, because they will slam the door shut:

- That person is all wrong for you. You need to break up with them.

- I'm not sure you should be dating them. This is not good.

- They are really controlling (or loud, annoying, narcissistic, etc.).

- I really think you should be dating Jan instead. She is such a cutie, and her mom says she likes you!

- I see all sorts of red flags here. Let's talk about them right now.

They will see the reality when they see it. Keep them talking and reflecting as much as you can. Of course, if you see signs of danger or abuse in the relationship, you will need to step in and tell it like it is quickly.

What Happened with Us

I loved what my girls did while they were "off the market" during the Covid-19 quarantine days. They came up with a list they called "The Sexy Seven" for when they were back in the dating world. This list had nothing to do with sex and everything to do with what they wanted in potential suitors once the world opened back up.

The list has served them well. They give a point for each of the seven qualities a guy exhibits to determine whether he is date worthy. They might give someone who scores less than a seven a chance (and a chance to improve his score). But come in at a five or below and you will not last long around here.

THE SEXY SEVEN

1. Must be a good person—someone who can put others before himself and has my best interest at heart.

2. Shows *no red flags,* such as
   - keeping our relationship a secret
   - demonstrating mental instability
   - talking to other girls (not just as friends)
   - manipulation
   - overall toxic behavior

3. Checks in on me and shows he cares about me.

4. Makes time for me.

5. Is a good communicator who can openly discuss both funny memes and serious emotions; is understanding, mature, not possessive or aggressive; and problem solves.

6. Lifts me up when I feel low and doesn't drag me down.

7. What I do for him equals what he does for me. It is a two-way street, and he should be putting the same amount of effort into the relationship as I do.

My youngest, Sam, would want you to know we also have something called the Little Brother Test. This one is simple: Will your significant other play Lego Star Wars with Sam? If it's a yes, they are in. Easy-peasy.

The Good News

Sometimes this part of teen life is so hard I want to (and have) put my head down on the table and sob. Yet this generation seems to think more about what they want in a relationship and less about just dating. They have thought through a screening process that they can revisit and change as they become more mature in their relationships with other humans. They are owning their responsibility to look at what they want and to ask for it.

Even if they are thinking through all the aspects, there is enormous pressure on our kids in relationships. We want to take that pressure off by reminding them that they are fearfully and wonderfully made and that the person they are dating is too. They should give the best, and they deserve the best. And if we let them know that should they need us, we are there waiting—without judgment but with curiosity and love—we might get front-row seats to their first loves. That also comes with seats at the table for heartbreak, which is when they really need us. It is hard, but you do not want to miss it.

Long Story Short

- Dating and falling in love can make teens a little crazy. That is normal, and they will do dumb things. It is all a part of it. If you expect this, you can be ready to handle it.

- You will have to talk about sex with your kids openly and honestly and without squirming. They need all the facts to keep their bodies and hearts safe.

- If your teen is in a bad breakup, empathy and sympathy are the order of the day. Watch for signs of depression if things are going on too long.

- Get to know the people your kids are dating, and help your teens reflect on their relationships.

- There can be a lot of pressure on our kids. We want them to be safe, so talk to them about their dating behavior early and often.

Dear Lord,

Please watch over our kids and those they are dating. Please help them know first that they are wonderful just as they are. Send significant others to my people who are exactly right for them. Help each one first build a friendship with their "dating partner" (I still don't have the cool term), and please let them listen to all we said about waiting to have sex and protecting their bodies. Help them see sex as the gift You have given us that is precious and not to be taken lightly.

Also help me stay open and listen with my head and my heart when they are talking to me about their love. We try to get it right, but we will fail too. Keep us close to You, and guide our words. And our kids' actions. All of them.

Amen.

CHAPTER 11

Teenagers in Church

Still Squirrelly and Also Questioning Their Faith

"Church is something for old people. If it were for teenagers, it would never be this early in the morning." One of my tall kids said this one Sunday as we were getting ready for church.

I stopped the hustle and the shoe hunt and the "Sam, go back up and put your socks on" that I was about to say.

I didn't know in that moment that God was working and that I would get shivers in the pew later that morning. But first . . .

"You guys, church is for you. I promise it is. The church needs you. You are the future of the whole thing, and without you God's message won't go on."

"But what if we find out later another religion totally different from ours was right and this is all for nothing?" said one.

"Yeah, and what if I become Hindu. Will God still love me?" asked another.

"The church needs your questions, and these are good ones that you can think about in church. God is big and mysterious, and none of us has it all right. That is impossible. And we go to church to sit in quiet to just know Him and to learn about Him and to thank Him. Also, it's only an hour, and we're leaving now, so put your shoes on and get in the car."

I feel this was a pretty good balance of discussing theology and getting people out the door on a Sunday morning.

We got to church, and the sermon was on—you guessed it—*this very topic.*

Well played, God.

As the pastor started talking to us about the church's stance on other religions, I turned around to make sure my people were listening, because clearly God was talking directly to them.

Our pastor talked about the love God has for all His people. And he pointed out that it is our job as Christians to show others the love and truth of our faith with our actions. We need to love others and come to the table with people who are different from us with hearts full of love.

And right in the bulletin was this quote:

> We need to put away the idea that we have a monopoly on the Truth and fully embrace the love God has for all of His children.

Bam.

That is the stuff that will keep our kids in church, friend. This generation is not interested in who is right. They are interested in truth. They know the truth is not simple, because their lives are not simple. And they are not going to be spoon-fed theology and then just believe it and move on.

What You Can't Do

We can lead our kids to church, but we can't make them pray. So then what? We can get their bodies there, but how can we keep their hearts engaged? The community we attend is so important.

In our family, we make it to church most Sundays, sit in the pew for a solid hour, grab doughnuts afterward (still a priority with the big kids), and then try and bake this experience into our week somehow.

Sometimes, this space after church is where we see some of the fruits of our early-Sunday-morning, giant labor. Because I believe our kids' hearts are hungry for Jesus, even if they don't know it. Once they are in church, the message has a chance to get in. We sometimes have deep talks about the week's message because they really care about these topics most of the time, even if young me would have never dared debate anything I heard at church. I was a taker-in-er, not a debater.

You see, I was a youth group kid. This is most likely not a shocker. I loved everything about it—singing, listening to the talks, going on the retreats, talking about the Bible, holding hands, and going to church with my friends. It was all my jam. If you needed me to lead a retreat table, I was there for you. *Can I give a talk too? Super!* Would I miss a big dance at school to be there? Absolutely. If you just signed me up for everything Jesus, I would listen to your Christian music, buy your Christian T-shirt, and wear my Youth Encounter cross with every single outfit I owned. I bought it all, and it was so lovely.

I was an accepter of all things. It all fit how God made me. I just wanted to have a good time and follow the rules. The more rules, the better, because rules made things super safe. So of course my kids would find this same joy in all these things, right?

Nope. You can't make your kids walk your same path. My kids were born question askers. And they didn't just save their questions for the limited time we had to get ready for church on a given Sunday.

I could keep up with answering them only until they got old enough to ask the really hard ones. I mean I could handle "Why do we have to go to church on Sunday instead of Thursday?" But then they started asking or saying things like this:

- "So, are you saying my Jewish friend is going to hell?"

- "But if everyone is made in God's image, aren't gay people in His image? Or are you saying God made some people wrong?"

- "If someone has an abortion or is divorced, are they kicked out of some of the things at church? And why would we kick them out? It would seem they might need God the most."

- "I learned in history that church leaders were super corrupt."

- "There are so many different religions. How can only one of them be right?"

Whew.

They are questioners who are looking to find God in all places. They are looking for a way to accept all people like I believe that God is actually calling all of us to do. These questions are not really about God so much as they are about us.

I did finally have to ask some questions around my own beliefs, which I realized weren't even really beliefs but only assumptions of my own rightness. It was time for me to study and read and talk to people outside my little circle—people of other denominations and ethnicities who had been brought up differently yet were loved by God and loved Him fiercely.

My teens challenged a lot of things—purity culture, patriarchy, and the rules and regulations—and it all led me back to my own relationship with Jesus. I had to get a little uncomfortable. Was I just trying to follow the rules and check the boxes so Jesus would love me and in turn them? In doing that, wasn't I saying I really didn't believe that He died for my sins, full stop? How did God love us? How could I show that love to my children through the way I loved them and the way we worshipped?

What You Can Do

You can question alongside them and deepen your own faith. This is exactly what happened for me. I realized that even if all the rules went away, God's love held. God loves us with this enormous unconditional love. I have made it through so many things only because I've been able to lean on Him in prayer and trust Him to hold me up. Having a relationship with God and Jesus and the Holy Spirit is the rock I cling to in the storms life brings.

The questions your teens ask might change some aspects about how you approach your own faith and relationship with God. This is an opportunity to grow. To listen. To question. God is big enough to take our questions. He is not afraid of them. And He isn't afraid of our teens' questioning either.

We do not have to have all the answers. We just need to be open and curious. God created this beautiful, complicated, and diverse world, and there are many ways to look at and experience His love for us. If there is even a chance that we can think about His Word and His love in other sound ways, shouldn't we be open to them?

I used to be so sure about what I considered the hard and fast rules, and now my heart is so much softer and my ears more open. I listen and think about their questions. I read the Bible on a loop because I know I want more for all of us when it comes to our faith. This next generation is not into looking shiny in church every Sunday and checking the boxes. If this is what we offer, they will take a hard pass and out into the world they will go. No wonder 57 percent of kids leave their faith before the age of eighteen.[4]

But if we are about our kids finding a deep, lasting faith and relationship with God that they can take with them everywhere, we must let them go and find that path. That is between them and God. And if I have to trust someone with my kids, God is the one I want to trust.

What if they find a faith and a connection to God that is deep but outside the walls of my church or denomination? I believe there is so much common ground we can agree on. We can love one another in the overlap. And I for one cannot wait to see what it is, talk to them about it, and walk alongside them there too.

What Happened for Us

We are still deep in the journey of faith, so check back in maybe ten years to see how this pans out in my kids' adulthood. I will say this: They remain open. They are exploring and finding themselves. One just said to me, "Mom, you being open and not having the answers is what is keeping me thinking I can believe in God. I don't have to believe in a religion and all of its rules." All I want for them in the world is to stay near to Him.

And just the other night, twenty-year-old Lily called me into her room and asked if I could give her "blessings." Blessings are how I used to tuck them in every night, when tucking in was a thing. So I did it like I had when she was little. I traced a little cross on her forehead, and I prayed over her. I prayed that she would have good sleep and a heart that felt peace and that God would help her with whatever she was worried about or struggling with. I prayed she would know how deeply she was loved. And I prayed it all "in Jesus's name, amen."

God's love holds. It is big enough for every single question and wondering—all of it. All. Of. It. And my heart was so happy that at that moment my tall baby was asking me to help her lean on the Lord.

The Good News

I believe with all my heart that all of God's paths will lead us to love. Our teenagers need to hear this message from us. They may not be easy paths. But there is room for every single one of us on this journey home to Him. Our prayers may look and sound different, but God hears them all. I want to teach my kids God is here for everyone. If a man-made rule doesn't match up with "The greatest of these is love,"[5] then we have to look a little more skeptically at that rule and err on the side of—you guessed it—love.

I am not a Bible scholar or a theologian. There are about a million people wiser than me in this arena. But I do know that when it comes to parenting our teenagers, if we want them to stay close to God, we need to remind them over and over how much God loves them and how much God wants us to bring our questions to Him. We need to encourage them that understanding the Bible and its context is a good thing and that even though it might make their questions multiply, they have their whole lives to keep asking and learning. We want to help them stay close to God and let Him do the rest. He loves our kids even more than we do, my friend. And that is an amazing and wonderful thing.

Long Story Short

- We have to leave room for our kids' questions and be open to learning with them. This is a great opportunity for us to get clear about our own faith.

- Find a church that will keep your kids coming with you, if you can. Make an agreement with them about their attendance prior to age eighteen, in particular, so they are at least a part of a community. It will keep them talking, even if they disagree with what they are hearing.

- God's love will hold. It is big enough for all our curiosity and questions. Trust it and trust Him.

- Remember that God loves our kids even more than we do. He will pursue them relentlessly. We need to remind them of this love.

Dear Lord,

Please guide our kids back to You. Let them know Your love and what that really means for them. Help them separate *You* from all the stuff the world says. Please grant us patience when they are still antsy in church or falling asleep on our shoulders. At least they are still there, and I know You appreciate the effort we are making even if our follow-through on sitting still is small.

Help our kids know You in deep, meaningful, and lasting ways, and help us step back so they can walk their own walks with You, even if that looks different than we thought it would or want it to. Remind us always that You love them more than we could ever know and that we can trust that love. Thank You for being big enough to handle our questions and curiosities and doubts. Help them feel Your love as we do.

All the amens.

CHAPTER 12

When Your Teenager Struggles with Mental Health

Things Just Got Serious and Really, Really Hard

"**M**om, I think I am dying."

I was sitting at a table in my office at the middle school. The room was bright and cheerful, with plants hanging from the ceiling and inspirational sayings all over the walls, and the teachers around me were chattering. I had been feeling so good and hopeful in this work.

I looked down at the words my kid had texted me, and my mind went quickly through all the things they could mean. I typed back, "What is going on???" knowing the multiple question marks would be considered aggressive.

I waited and stared at those three little dots as the conversation continued to flow around me. Finally the message came through. "I am in the bathroom. I can't breathe. I think I might be having a heart attack. It's so bad, Mom. Come get me."

Immediately I was pretty sure I knew what we were dealing with. My heart sank, realizing it was happening to another of my kids. "I think you are having a panic attack. Go to the health room and tell them that you think this is what is happening. Can you do that? I'll meet you there."

"KK" was the reply.

Then I did that thing all working parents have experienced: I quickly explained to my co-workers that we had a kid in crisis and left the meeting with all my stuff still on the table. They understood and supported me and were amazing.

I rushed over to the high school to guide this child through the panic attack. I also called the doctor to make a plan for this kid.

At this point in my parenting, I had experience in dealing with my kids and panic attacks. But the first time it happened, it caught me completely off guard.

It started with our oldest, who was a born performer. She loved putting on shows as a little girl. She hit the real stage at the age of five, playing a flying monkey in a production of *The Wizard of Oz*. She was hooked. She auditioned and performed in whatever she could, all the way into her high school years, and we were so proud. She seemed to be living her dream.

So it made zero sense to my brain when she stood up to sing a solo at a high-school-level competition and just froze. She stood there, looking terrified, with eyes wide and skin growing paler by the second. I sat helplessly as she stammered, "I think I am going to pass out." That gave me permission to jump up and finally go to her like I was dying to. I took her arm and led her out of the room and into the hallway.

Her breathing was shallow and fast. I put my hand on her back and told her to breathe with me. "In and out, sweet girl, in and out. Breathe with me. You've got this."

I honestly thought maybe she had just locked her knees (that's a thing, right?) or needed a snack. I had no idea this was the beginning of something deeper. As we walked through the halls and tried to help her breathe, we happened to run into a friend from her days on the stage in community theater. When we explained what had happened, she said, "That sounds like an anxiety attack. It's going to be really important that you go back and compete today. You have to tell your body it can do this." She spent another minute with us, reinforcing the idea of breathing, and then was on her way.

We were happy to have some actionable advice, so we breathed and prepped, and somehow she made it through her last song. I didn't want to believe it was anything more than a blip. I wanted everything to be okay. I wanted her to be able to perform. I wanted her to hold on to this identity that, frankly, I had become attached to. I wanted her to be able to keep up with her dreams.

Yet the hits kept coming. First whenever she had to sing in front of people. Then at auditions. And then when she was just sitting in the car waiting to walk into school. In no time at all, I went from trying to help her hold on to her dream to helping her just get through a day at a functioning level. It all unraveled so fast. And I didn't know why.

Instead of things playing out like all the other times my kids were sick, this time the child wanted nothing—not a bed made up on the couch or a special treat or her favorite movie. Nothing except to be left utterly and totally alone.

I was terrified in my soul.

It took months and several visits to the doctor to navigate the biology of what was happening, as well as appointments with counselors who helped with therapy and strategies for dealing with it. Slowly but surely we made progress and healing happened.

Now it was starting again, this time with a different child. But this time I knew more.

Just like I couldn't keep any of my kids from having an appendicitis attack, needing their tonsils out, or even spraining a finger on a Build-A-Bear (true story), I couldn't keep mental illness away either.

Before my kids reached their teenage years, I had always thought good parenting, open communication, and acceptance of these people just as God made them could ward off *anything* that would trouble their minds.

Apparently, biology and minds don't work that way.

What You Can't Do

I have learned that you can't love kids out of a panic attack any more than you can love them out of strep throat.

You can't pray them out of a broken leg, and you can't pray them out of depression.

But you *can* be there. You can try to understand what they need next, even if it's not as easy as a Popsicle to soothe their aching throats. You can entrust them to medical professionals like you did when their appendix almost burst, and you can walk alongside them to make sure they take their medication and to help them learn how their bodies work and to get well.

Having a teenager means you can be sitting after dinner, playing a little Hay Day on your phone, and suddenly you will nearly get knocked off the couch by a child who dives into your lap, forgetting they are not in a five-year-old body. Their next sentence may just be "I'm so tired, and I really want Chick-fil-A, and they are closed!" or it may be something like "Mom, I need to tell you something. I have been cutting. For months. I need help. Please help me. I don't know what's wrong."

The uncertainty of mental illness can put us in a state of high alert, fear, and worry. We know this doesn't make us our best selves. I try to remind myself of Deuteronomy 31:8, where

God tells us not to be afraid because He goes before us always. But remembering that God goes before you is very hard when you are stricken in your heart about what your baby is going through, knowing you cannot protect them.

I remember one night being consumed with worry about one of our people. Little by little she had school problems and friend problems, and we watched her mental health tank—first at school, then at work, and soon essentially anywhere and anytime.

I felt I was watching my happy-go-lucky, laid-back kid disappear in front of my eyes, and I couldn't save her.

The middle of the night would come, and the fear and worry would consume me. I would turn to the Lord and beg Him to protect my baby, who was in her room as always, with the door closed and her blankets pulled up over her head.

I would check in as much as allowed, but doing so too many times seemed to only make it worse. All I wanted to do with every single fiber of my being was to tuck my baby back in my bed, right between me and my husband, and hold her hand while she slept.

This was not a thing for this kid. She needed to suffer alone, privately, with no one watching at all. This is the exact opposite of how I choose to suffer. (See again chapter 5, "I Am Not Parenting Myself.")

What You Can Do

You can be there with your kids, believe them, and support them. Always. After the last check-in of the night when everyone in the house was asleep but me, I quietly snuck my blanket and pillow out of my room and slept in front of my daughter's door so that if she tried to leave or found herself in need, I would be right there and wouldn't miss it.

It was the only thing I could do—get as close to her pain as possible and hope to absorb some of it through her door. I would pray myself to sleep on the hard hallway floor, and if I was lucky, a cat would curl up on my feet to keep me company.

If you find yourself in a similar place—praying, hoping, willing a way to absorb your child's pain—you will wonder how you ended up here. You will wonder what happened to the child you used to know. You will doubt every single parenting move you have made thus far.

But the night lies to you. That child is still there, and so is a brand-new almost adult who is trying to figure out the big issues of life. You cannot fix adult things as easily as you could fix child things. Finding a lost blankie or gluing Buzz Lightyear's wings back on was easy. This stuff... not at all.

The love I had for them was my driving force when things got so dark. Love couldn't fix it, but it could be there to remind them they were not alone. And I could keep offering them that love without a single condition. Without a single drop of judgment. With nary an expectation. Without ceasing. When they need something in their lives that will hold no matter what? It can be our love.

So, that is what I did. Love is what I did on the hard hallway floor.

If you find yourself needing help to navigate the rough waters of your kid's mental health struggles, you can lie on that hallway floor in the night. But then when the morning comes, you will need to get up and make a get-that-kid-into-therapy call. You may also find yourself explaining in-depth to the receptionist—not even the therapist, mind you—that "my kid has always been wonderful, and I have no idea why this is happening. Can you get us in right away, because this is not normal and I'm terrified and . . . Why, yes, we do have insurance, and yes, I'll hold." Deep exhale. Now breathe.

You may feel frantic and afraid to make that call. Perhaps you're worried about what everyone would think if they knew your kid doesn't want to get out of bed in the morning and is failing their classes. Or that to get them anywhere, you have to drive a shaking human all the way to the destination and then hope they don't bolt in a full-on panicky sweat.

You may find yourself caught between pushing your teen out to live a "normal" life and wanting them to be in your house where they prefer to be—while also worrying about how much time they seem to spend all alone and how little they will say to you about any of it.

It is all such new territory that you will feel just as lost as you did the first time your baby cried all night long or had their first fever or lost their first friend.

But the thing is, *you are not supposed to fix this.* Of course, your heart will tell you that you need to fix every bit of it. It is your job as a mother, right? Your baby is suffering! Making their struggles stop seems to be your whole reason for being on earth.

Except now it isn't. Not anymore. They have to work through the unfixable. Because they are not only our children; they are also human beings who have their own paths to walk, paths we cannot possibly smooth out or walk for them. Sometimes there will be very little room on their paths for us to even walk beside them. We may have to stand a distance away shouting our encouragement and hoping they hear through the storm that is raging around them as they walk. We can yell our love at them and hold up signs that remind them our love is here. We have to let them become themselves, even when being honest is so hard.

It is even less fun than it sounds.

This may sound like the voice of someone who has it all figured out, but it is actually the voice of someone once again lying on the floor outside a teenager's door at night because that is the closest I can get to him right now. I need to be near him in the same way I needed to rock him all night when he had a fever as a baby, but now that isn't quite what he needs. He needs space, so outside his door praying without ceasing is where I need to be.

When your teenager's body or mind seems to turn against them, it is the most helpless feeling in the world. The stakes are so high. They have enough independence that they can get out of your sight, and then what? It's terrifying.

And when they had strep throat? Well, I could post about our misery on Facebook and get all sorts of "I hope they feel better soon" or "Have you tried throwing away their tooth-brushes?" messages. But when their minds are hurting, there is no Facebook post you can make. And if you do post about it, you might get answers that seem to have hidden messages with whispers of shame.

It's very, very lonely. And very, very hard.

And very, very common, as it turns out.

So many of us have suffering kids—or are suffering ourselves—and we flat-out don't talk about it. Yet it is just as commonplace as having a kid who needs knee surgery because they overworked it in basketball. Some of our kids have minds and hearts that have been overworked or are just made in such a way that everything becomes a struggle.

What Happened for Us

There was a day I walked into my girl's room and two sisters were cuddled around a sobbing third. They looked me in the eyes and told me she had something to say.

When she couldn't stop crying to tell me, I asked whether she was okay with her sisters saying it. She was. My middle girl looked at me with sympathy and love (she is a future psy-chologist, and I swear she was born for it) and said, "Mom, she isn't eating. She can't. We are pretty sure she has an eating disorder. She said she tried to fix it and just can't do it. We have to get her help."

Suddenly we were called to fight against an invisible mon-ster whispering in my girl's ears that she wasn't good enough. I knew social media was bombarding these kids with all the messages about how they are not good enough just as they are. But I had told my kids for years and years, "You are as God made you. You are beautiful and perfect in His image." I tried not to make food a thing, and I didn't talk about dieting or working out in front of them. And still, the one thing my kids heard was that invisible monster whispering to them that they needed to make themselves smaller.

Now, there were many complex reasons we ended up in this spot—things having to do with control and their place in the world. It was all complicated and hard, and we needed profes-sional people to help us untangle it. It was hard to share with our world. But when we did, we found out we were not alone. So many others were struggling with this alongside us.

Our world is broken, but so often we feel like we cannot admit being broken ourselves. I have found this to be true when other people whisper to me about their struggles and when I struggle to share my own.

Why are we like this?

We think we are living completely abnormal broken lives, yet *everyone's* life is broken in some way. By its very definition, this means it is completely normal to live a broken life. We are humans. We break easily in our bodies, our minds, and our hearts. And for some reason, we want to give awards to people who don't break—or at least who pretend they don't break.

And we all chase it. In the meantime, we hide our brokenness from one another and are lonely and miserable, and we shush our children, telling them not to say a thing about their own brokenness, making the next generation feel this same way.

I am here to tell you that it is okay to be broken. It is okay to talk about being broken. It is okay for our kids to be broken. It is okay for our kids to talk about being broken. And in that moment in the bedroom, this is what I told my kids.

Brokenness is normal, and when it happens, we need to find out why and not ignore any of it. I tell them this as I drag them to therapy. I will no more ignore the pains of their minds and souls than I will of their bellies or their throats.

I will not tell them to suck it up. I will not let them hide from the pain. I will not let them for one moment think they are abnormal weirdos for the pains of their minds and hearts and souls. They are gloriously human, and they are feeling all their feels, just as they should. They can be both broken and whole. Because the only way to be whole is to accept your brokenness.

And the only way to the other side of suffering is through it. But they have what it takes to make it through. And they can be open and honest about it, even if it is hard and they feel like it is not what someone wants to hear.

I fear I did say "You are fine. Suck it up" way more than I should have in their early years. And, yes, sometimes we do need to suck it up. But sometimes we are sucking it up while we are *not* fine. Our kids need us to help them *stop* sucking it up.

How do they still participate in life when they are going through hard things? How do they pull themselves up and out of the pit when hard things become a part of their stories? And how do we stay steady and true so they can use us as one of those rocks to pull themselves up?

Notice I didn't ask how *we* pull them out of it. Because the really, really hard truth is that we can't. They have to do the work. We can provide the tools, the space, and the support, but this work is theirs. Once we make peace with that, we can help them in very meaningful ways. But if we make it about us, it is way harder to provide that support.

Talk early, talk often, and take the stigma, silence, and secrecy out of mental health struggles. Kids should be able to come to us not only with broken toes but also with overwhelming feelings of anxiety that won't let up. And we should look for professionals to help us when both of these things happen. I mean, I do know how to splint a toe, but assuming I can handle this alone and without an X-ray (as I may have done once—another mistake) may mean a really sore foot and longer healing for the kid. The same goes for mental health struggles: Do not try to lead them out of it alone.

The Good News

When I was a teenager, *mental health* was not a term I ever heard mentioned. Now my twelve-year-old often asks people how their mental health is, and he really wants to know. The world has changed, and teens are going through so much more. We are more aware of things we once thought were rare, like anxiety and depression, as our kids are living in a more complex world. Many of us have found the tools we need for our own mental health, and we are handing them down to our kids. Or maybe we are seeing how this is working and healing for them and they are handing the tools up to us. Either way, it is a new generation of a deeper understanding of our minds, bodies, and hearts.

It is normal for our kids to have some down days and to not want to talk sometimes. But if these feelings go on for a long time without improving, if their feelings don't make sense or seem extreme, if they are not handling their emotions well, or if they are coping in unhealthy ways, it is not normal and they may need professional help. When in doubt, reach out. It can never hurt. If you are concerned about suicide, ask. This does not plant the seed of the idea in your teen's head. It opens the door for conversation. And if they mention suicide, always take this seriously.

We need to all look out for one another. I talked with a friend recently who was dealing with her child's mental health struggles. She spent the entire previous night trying to fix things. They had been on this road for a long time, but no one at all knew. When it reached its peak and super difficult decisions were made, this parent still showed up for work the next day because she felt like the whole thing needed to be set aside on a shelf so no one would see that the problem existed.

This person showed up for work and tried to be . . . normal.

When nothing in her world was *normal* at all.

How many of us have done this?

When my kid's appendix almost burst, I had to rush out in the middle of a meeting. I took three days off to sit with her in the hospital, and I came back to forty emails wishing her well.

Yet when I listened to my friend's story, I knew I might do the exact same thing she had done if it were my kid. Given the option of showing up to work or telling the truth, I would probably rather just show up because sharing this truth wouldn't feel very freeing in our current world.

When our kid's behavior or feelings are in the not-normal category, though, we have to take action. We have to work to get them the help they need. We need to monitor them to be sure their medications and therapy are doing the trick. We might have to sit with them through breakdowns and pray we get to be there for the breakthroughs. It is hard. There is no way to shine it up and put a bow on it, friend. When your kid struggles with mental health, it's hard and scary and you are allowed to feel afraid. But know you are not alone. Hope and life are on the other side. I will make it, and you will too.

Long Story Short

- We cannot love our kids out of mental health troubles, just like we cannot love them out of a cold or strep throat. We need to get them proper help.

- "Good parenting" may not keep your child from mental health struggles. This is not your fault, nor is it your child's fault. We need to keep shame out of this arena.

- Be there to walk beside them, reminding them that you love them unconditionally and that God does too.

- We must be there when they need us while also giving them space. We must also be watchful for when they need more help than they are getting.

- We need to take the misconceptions and stigma out of mental health struggles, anxiety attacks, eating disorders, cutting, addiction, and all the other battles our kids go through.

- Take care of yourself when your child is struggling. You may also find you are having similar problems or need additional help in order to support them. Getting your child to the therapist and then yourself to one can be a very healing and healthy thing.

Dear Lord,

The times our kids struggle are the hardest. Please remind us You are with us. Please hold us close and hold them too. Give us the words we need to talk about really hard things, to ask for help, and to share our struggles in safe spaces. Please send us humans to walk beside us who will be these safe spaces. Help us help our kids in all the ways they need. Let us discern the moments when they need us most, and let us see all the opportunities to lead them from darkness into the light.

Please bring peace to our hearts, Lord, reminding us You love our kids as well and that You will use our struggles for good. Help move our world to be more understanding of all the parts of our humanity. Let us be as open with the struggles of our minds and souls as we are with those of our bodies. Help us to be understanding and supportive of those around us all the time. Let our kids know they can come to us with all the things just as we can come to You. Be with us in the night while we lie outside bedroom doors and with the children on the other side of those doors who desperately need You.

All the amens.

CHAPTER 13

Letting Go

(Yes, You Do Have To)

A short video popped up on my feed today of a girl, maybe four or five years old, on her little purple two-wheeled bike. She was riding in her parents' driveway, a pink helmet on her head, her ponytail sailing out the back, and a big grin on her face. She went out of the driveway and straight on down the block, having so much fun. Her mom captioned the picture, "Took the training wheels off today and she just rode away."

I realized this was exactly what it looked like to launch our kids out into the world the day they moved out of our house for the first time. We had been their training wheels for years, keeping them upright and safe and going in the right direction, keeping them from tipping over and getting hurt. Then all at once we had to remove ourselves; we had to let them try life on their own. And when we let go, each of them just rode away. It felt like our job here was done, at least for a hot minute. We could be there to help them up if they fell, but they would be taking on the world by themselves. Yet that moment they rode away . . . Oh man, they each took a piece of my heart with them. And when someone chips off a piece of your heart, it hurts a little.

I had a lot of big, sad feelings when my girls went to college. I can still put myself back in those moments.

We had spent the day loading up Ellie's dorm room, exploring her campus, and eating an awesome lunch together as a family. Then it came—the moment we had tried to pretend wasn't going to happen but was the reason we were there. The leaving.

I can see all of us lining up to give Ellie hugs, then loading into the minivan, her seat now empty as a reminder of what this day was about. We all rolled down our windows and waved wildly, my hair bigger than ever from the stress of it all and continually sticking to my face in my tears.

We drove away. The way she stood there so sad, waving and trying to be brave, is burned into my brain forever. I got myself together only to look over at Todd, who was sobbing as he steered the car onto the highway. Of course I lost it again, only to turn around and see every kid in the car in tears. Good grief, we can be a feeling people.

When we left Lily at school two years later, I thought I was better prepared. I was happy for her actually. She had lost so much during the pandemic. But nope, all the tears again. I sobbed the entire way back into our driveway like a crazy person. I can wallow right there in the beautiful sadness of it all.

What We Can't Do

We cannot escape the variety of emotions letting go will bring. Yes, for me there were sadness and sweet goodbyes. However, a whole bunch of other emotions had led up to this. And some of them were not great.

I was looking through my computer one day and found something entitled "Expectations for Living in Our House Senior Year." It propelled me back into the moments that felt less like sadness and much more like fury and frustration, together with an understanding of why birds shove their babies out of the nest when it is time for them to fly. Those birds are onto something, I can tell you that. There were days when I would have easily set the child and her stuff on the curb and shouted, "If you are so smart, then just figure it out on your own!" and I would have walked away guilt-free.

I have included that list here so you can see pretty much where my headspace was the year before she left. I am mortified that I typed this up and likely printed it out and handed it to her. Like, *Yes, Amy, that is the exact way to fix this situation. Just type it up and hand it to her. Then she will understand and do everything the right way.* Clearly, I wanted to control something, but alas, this memo might as well have been written in disappearing ink. It made a zero percent difference in our relationship and can go squarely in the "do not bother trying this strategy" column.

Please note my positive tone and can-do attitude throughout this document. Bonus points to me for trying:

Expectations for Living in Our House Senior Year

We are here for you, and we are looking forward to supporting you through this next year of your life.

While it can be filled with fun, there is also a lot for you to manage. We are happy to help, support, encourage, and love you through this time.

But . . . there will be some expectations placed on you. For some time I think we have sent the message that you can't do these things, that there is too much pressure on you and that you are not up to the task. That could not be further from the truth. You can do this. Here are some of the things we will be helping and supporting you with this year.

1. *You will contribute to the family.* This will include the things we ask of your siblings (chores, attending family functions) as well as some things that the adults in the family do as you are approaching adulthood (manage your own money, pay for gas in the car, make meals, etc.). There may be exceptions to this when times get really busy or tough. We will all pitch in to help each other when needed and should do so happily.

2. *You will manage your own money.* We will help you figure out how much you should be spending and saving each month. You will start to track your spending to determine how to best manage your money. You will save money for extras and for your future.

3. *You will balance your home/family/friend/job/school life.* This will include time for play and for rest. If you are always exhausted at home, then that is a sign you are going out too much.

4. *You will manage your own medications and care for your body.* If you need a pill box, buy one and be sure you are taking your meds. *Every day.*

5. *You will plan for your future.* I don't care what the plan is, but you are responsible for making it. We are happy to help you as you take the lead in your own life. You will research schools if you want to attend them, jobs if this is what you prefer, tests you need to take (such as the ACT). I will sit with you anytime, anyplace, and figure this out with you if you would like. I can't do this for you.

6. *You will hand schoolwork in on time and maintain a B or better average.* When you are missing assignments or your grades fall below this, your social life will be impacted.

7. *You will manage your job.* Asking for hours that you need off in a timely fashion, making sure you have transportation for your job well in advance (this means we will need to know your schedule), letting us know if you don't need a ride home before we show up, etc.

These might seem reasonable on some level, but the problem with presenting her with this list was that she *didn't know how* to do many of these things. I forgot to assume she was doing the best she could and instead tried to nicely outline all the ways she was failing. I didn't include her in the creation of the list or ask her how it was going or what was hard or easy for her. Instead, I wrote it using my good teacher language and handed it over. Also, that positive tone is pretty passive-aggressive when I look at it from her viewpoint, and I am not at all surprised that her attitude in return might have been "We'll see about that!"

The best shining up in the world cannot overcome a stubborn and unyielding heart, like mine certainly was at that time. We were caught in a push-and-pull power struggle over everything. In some ways this made it easier to say goodbye; it felt like it was time for her to go. And in other ways it made things so much harder—how could I let her go when there was so much between us left unresolved?

What You Can Do

You can soften your heart and communicate with your kid. I definitely should have softened both my heart and my expectations. I should have started with all the things she was doing well, finding and praising the good that was right there in my girl, rather than focusing only on what she needed to be doing to please us. I should have included her as a partner in thinking through her changing role in the family instead of parenting her like she was two while expecting her to act like an adult. This is so hard because we are so worried and just want to organize it all in a way that works. But you cannot organize someone else into submission.

If I could go back in time, I might have started with a letter instead of a list. And it might have looked a little something like this:

> **Dear sweet child of mine,**
>
> I see you are really no longer a child. Instead you are an almost adult, on the brink of so much change. I know this is such an exciting time and that people might expect you to be doing and thinking certain things, and I want you to know it's okay if you don't just feel excited and joyful. This can also be a conflicting and sad and overwhelming time. You are entitled to feel what you feel—and don't be surprised if you have all these feelings at once.
>
> Your dad and I want to support you through this time, but sometimes it is hard for us to get used to you

being so independent. We are used to knowing where
you are and who you are with and what you are doing, so
giving that up will take getting used to. We are also feeling all the feelings at once. Even though we are grown-
ups, we have never launched a grown-up, so it is all new
for us too. Please be patient when we have a hard time
letting you go. We are trying so hard.

We know you are trying, too, and your changing role
in the family probably feels a little strange. As you get
more independence, you are expected to have more responsibility. We will ask new things of you. We will ask
the old things of you too. You might feel busier and un-
able to balance it all. We are here to help you with that.
We want you to have the skills you need to be on your
own, and sometimes we may overwhelm you with too
many things. Know we can talk about that. We can always work something out so that you can have a clean
bathroom and complete homework and a weekend with
friends. It might take some time and compromise, but we
can help you get there. You will need these skills throughout your life, and each year you will get better at them. I
promise.

I'm sorry if we sometimes hold on too tight, and I'm
sorry if I sometimes say the wrong thing. I can get really
worried and scared, and when I speak from this place, I
say the thing in my heart that scares me instead of the
thing in my heart that is hopeful. I am working on that—
it's a me-thing, not a you-thing. It's never your job to be
sure I am happy and worry-free. I have to take care of
that. You have enough going on, sweet girl.

And know always, always, always, we think you are
capable and kind and talented and smart and flat-out
amazing. We know you can tackle whatever life throws at

you. And whenever you need support, we are here for you, cheering you on and ready to help in any way we can. It's okay to need help. You can be capable and confused at the same time. I know that, because that's how I am pretty much every single day. Reach out when you need it. You've got this.

This year might be hard and take a lot of figuring things out, but we can do this. We can both learn to balance the holding on and the letting go. We can figure out how you can have a curfew and a good time. We can make this year fun and full of learning while we also feel all the sad or hard feelings. We love you from the absolute bottoms of our hearts.

—Mom and Dad

That letter is so much better than the list that it breaks my heart a little. A letter is an invitation for feelings and conversation and openness. A list is something you check off in order to win or fail. And we never want our kids to think our love or their acceptance is based on a list of things they must do.

But, alas, I was at list level back in the day. Your teen's entire last year of high school is a roller coaster: You want to crack down on all the ways they are pulling against you while you're simultaneously feeling all the giant emotions of the "lasts" and agonizing over their plans for that weekend, let alone for the future.

There were so many feelings as we began looking ahead to our girl's future outside the walls of our family home. She and I sat one day at a coffee shop filling out college applications and imagining all the places she could be living the next year. We talked about the kind of people she hoped to meet and ideas she was starting to have about what her future might look like after college ended. This was the dream phase, and it did feel dreamy. We could see all she had worked for, so nearly within her grasp.

Then it would all fall to pieces when she stayed out way past her curfew and forgot to send in college deposits, and I wondered how this kid would survive. With both my girls I felt all these phases, but I will admit the second time around was much easier because I knew not to take it personally. And that second pancake had learned how to walk the walk from watching her sister. It helped.

Our third pancake has no desire or need to go yet, and that is wonderful and something I likely should have been more open to with my first. I was too worried about what people would say and about whether both of us would make it out alive should she stay home for another year. I now realize it matters zero percent what other people are doing or what they think. Our third child needs time to grow and figure out what he wants to do while having those training wheels on just a little bit longer. He is going to try out different jobs that align with the fields he is looking into, buy his own car, and do a whole bunch of things we couldn't even guess right now until the time comes for him to head out of our door. We are here for it.

No matter what their plans are after high school, we can find the good and the next possible step that is right *for them*. We are here to help them be who they are meant to be and not care a bit about what it looks like to anyone else.

What Happened for Us, Part One

The summer before each girl left for school, I spent all the minutes vacillating between wanting to hold on to her leg and never let her leave and also wanting to toss her in the car, drive her to school, and turn around and go home without looking back. Sometimes I felt both of these ways in the same minute.

The pain of those first nights away was shockingly agonizing for both of us. I missed her under my roof in a visceral way. It was so different than when she spent a night or two with friends or at a sleepover. It was knowing that she was moving on and that the nights she slept in her own bed would be fewer than those spent away. It was the symbolism of her being in her own new space and the realization that there would be *so much* I wouldn't know. *What if something happens and she 'doesn't come back to the dorm one night? Would anyone even know? What if she gets sick and needs something? What if she is scared and can't sleep? Did I even make sure she packed enough pillows?* I lay awake until all hours, and it turns out she did too.

Even for this first pancake who "couldn't wait to get out of this house!" the transition was hard. I needed to get past my own emotions fast so I could ground myself and help with hers. It is so hard not to jump on the train of their emotions and feel all their feels plus yours.

She would call us saying, "I hate it here. I have no friends, and I just really need to come home." She would cry. I would encourage. And try not to worry. And wait to see if she would find her people. Maybe she would try getting to know her roommate or ask someone to go down to dinner. But nothing seemed to be working.

Then one day Ellie hit a wall. She was sick and alone with no one to turn to. There were more tears and wanting to come home. She felt so alone—I could feel it across the miles in my soul. Every single fiber of my being wanted to get in the car, put the pedal to the metal, and get to my baby and hug her and tell her I was there for her and she could come home and live with me forever.

But, alas, this thing you really want to do is so often the exact thing you should not do. I knew rescuing her during this crucial time would send the message that she indeed could not do it. That she needed to be rescued. It was so hard to coach her from afar, reminding her that she could do this, and that it would be hard only for a short time. And then it happened. Little by little she did meet people. She used the hard times as motivation to find a new roommate and then gathered a little group of friends by her side. We stopped hearing from her around the clock. And by Christmas break she didn't even want to come home. Sweet relief. Believe me, I swear they will not be lonely and friendless forever.

Of course, you know your child. If you see your person spiraling downward in their mental health, if this period of friendless blues seems to last way longer than it should, or if you can just tell something is off deep in their soul, then go and check on them if you need to. But in 95 percent of the cases, friends, comfort, and stability are right on the other side of that call. Your child will find what they need if they decide to stick it out and try to find their place in this whole baffling world.

We should not steal their opportunity to live through this and do the work that leads to their growth. That moment they find they have made a friend or forced themselves to join a club or an activity is the moment they feel so empowered and capable. They get to know they can make it through hard times. They learn empathy for those who are struggling, and they also try to make sure no one feels friendless in the way they did. So much growth happens during this time, but it comes at a cost to our sleep. There is no denying that.

What Happened for Us, Part Two

The second pancake left, and it was like a dream. She immediately found so many friends! She loved it! She had all sorts of things to do! The end. I had figured it out, right?

Nope.

The friends she found were all the wrong ones. Like *really* bad. She veered toward the flashiest, most dramatic group as a default as she leaned full-on into her newfound freedom.

We saw red flags everywhere we looked, but she was thrilled and finding herself. We gently tried to suggest keeping herself open to meeting other new people. We prayed. I kept myself from driving there and popping in on the whole situation. We prayed some more. But it turned out that, soon enough, she was seeing the red flags too. All the talking we had done about friends for the last eighteen years had stuck. Our parenting had stuck. Her trust in herself had stuck. And I will always, always be thankful to God above that she listened to those little voices inside herself and realized this was no good.

It was a gift that she had the opportunity to take those training wheels off and just zip right away and find what she didn't want to be a part of all on her own. She went on to find the most amazing group of buddies after this struggle. While we could say every drop of worry was wasted because it all turned out okay, it was an opportunity for me to realize again that living in worry and fear is not the answer—and to acknowledge that I didn't need to reach out and steady her. I coached from the sidelines, and I was getting it. I was growing, too, as it turned out. Go, me.

While I am excited and ready for the third pancake to stay home, we are now trying to navigate life after high school with a new set of challenges. We have to decide with him what his leveling up to adulthood will look like. He will need something to be responsible for, something that will hold him accountable and give him the pride that comes with contribution. He will enter the workforce in a job designed for grown-ups, which will bring all sorts of new and different lessons for him to learn. Although we are lucky to get a front-row seat to this, at times that feels a little too close for all of us.

We still want him to know he can fail and come to us when he does. And he will need more freedom while he's under our roof, which is a different kind of challenge. Because he is a different kid. Each one of our people needs us to show up in the way that fits them best. I am proud of him for pausing at this point, and I am so happy the world is beginning to understand that college isn't the be-all and end-all for every graduate.

The Good News

We are guiding our kids into adulthood and then setting them free to test it all out. It is the hardest and most natural thing in the world, and it feels totally wrong and completely right at the same time. Is it any wonder we struggle? Or maybe some of us don't. Maybe we feel joy and happiness and freedom at their launch. That is a wonder too. We get to feel our feelings, whatever they are, with no judgment. Each of us is on our own journey. May we stand collectively and look in wonder at our people as they bravely go into the world. May we lean on one another where we can, always ready to help our kids on the next step in their journey. And may they know they can always, always come home where they are loved beyond measure.

Long Story Short

- Expect to want to hold on tight one minute and kick them to the curb the next. It's normal.

- Try to keep a stance of love and connection, even in those kick-to-the-curb moments.

- It may get harder before it gets easier.

- The first nights and weeks can be tough. Don't rescue them unless you have big mental health concerns.

- Don't get on the roller coaster of emotions.

- Each kid is different. Help them find the path that makes the most sense for them. Do not compare.

- Feel your feelings, and look at them in wonder. They are doing it!

Dear Lord,

Please hold our children close as we leave them in all the places and drive away as they walk into dorms and apartments and have to do life on their own. Let our hugs not be too crushing, and let our tears not make them worry that we think they won't survive. Rather, let them know those tears mean they are truly and deeply loved.

Help us drive away and not swing back around because we "forgot something" when we really want to see them for one more second. Help us in the dead of the night when we are thinking about all the things we forgot to say. Help us realize that they know enough to get through and that we can always call them tomorrow to remind them how much detergent to put in the wash and to be sure they have enough pillows.

When they are really sad and homesick, help us discern whether it is a real problem or they just need time to get themselves into this new world. Let us support them from afar and pray over them from our own homes. I believe our prayers can stretch just like our hearts. Help us guide them where we can and remind them we are there for them no matter what weird thing happens while they are away. Love them for us, Lord, in the night when they are lonesome. And as always, guide them in Your footsteps and not in those of the person down the hall going to all the parties. Thank You, Lord.

Amen.

CHAPTER 14

The First Coming Back, and So It Goes

If you want to see what joy looks like in human form, come and stand in my entryway when a kid comes home from college. It is like all of us turn into puppies and we run and hug and tumble.

That first homecoming is the sweetest moment. When my baby walked back in those doors for the first time after being away, I exhaled so fully I realized I had been holding my breath a little since we had left her behind at school. Every single sibling ran to her and crushed her into the most beautiful group hug I have ever seen. It felt so good to just look at her. We all gathered around and shared stories. I was so pumped for the four days of Thanksgiving break and all the fun we would have. All my people were home, and all was right with the world.

I remember sitting on our couch relaxing after starting a load of her laundry and helping her get settled. I was talking to Todd about what movie we might all watch. I had dreams of the family cuddled up on the couch with a movie and popcorn, my girl's head on my shoulder, when I noticed her heading into the bathroom with a change of clothes and her makeup bag.

"Are you getting ready for bed already?" I asked, confused.

"What? Nope, it's only nine. I'm getting ready to go out. Everyone is home, and we are all meeting up at someone's house. I think it's a sleepover, but I'll be home in the morning. I'm so excited to see everyone!"

She shut the bathroom door before she could see my face fall. I couldn't believe it. She was leaving already? And without asking? I mean, I got it, but still. And she was excited to see everyone, but weren't *we* everyone?

The dream of a whole-family movie night vanished.

The fact she was super excited to see her friends was completely understandable and normal. I tried to brush it off, but then I had to remind myself that my reaction was understandable and normal too. I was allowed to be sad and disappointed she wasn't home. But I also needed to own those feelings and keep myself from putting them on her.

What We Can't Do

We cannot go back in time and return to how things were. I'm sure I failed in this department on this night. I am sure I said, "I wish you were staying home. We miss you so much, and I can't believe you are leaving us already." And I'm sure I ruined her night a little for no good reason other than to relieve my feelings.

I'm much better now, and it took only a few years of practice. This week my sweet secondborn was home for barely twenty-four hours when she left for an overnight stay with a friend. I am proud to say I helped her pick out a fun outfit, gave her a hug, and said I missed her and couldn't wait to hear all about their adventures. I felt sad, but I am no longer disappointed, because I know the deal. They have whole, big lives outside these walls. If I want them to continue to make this home a place they enjoy coming to where they can completely relax and be themselves, I need to be sure there is room for those big lives they are living.

Those big lives might mean they have new ways of being and doing things. They may come home and no longer eat meat when you had planned burgers for the family meal. Grab a pack of their favorite veggie burgers, or ask them for a recipe they enjoy that you can all try together. They may dress differently than they did. Compliments on their new look, even if it is the exact thing you never wanted to see them wear, will always be welcome. They are trying on all different ways of being, and we are here for that. We are applauding that. We are complimenting that.

Remember when they first went to school and fell in love with their teacher and suddenly that teacher had all the wisdom and we didn't always know the right things anymore? Or remember when their new friend Cindy liked Daniel Tiger, so everything had to be Daniel Tiger just like that new pal? This is like that, but sometimes it involves tattoos.

We need to get excited for all the newness, even if the newness isn't what we would pick. We have a saying in our home: "Don't yuck someone's yums." You may need to play this on a loop if your big comes home with new food, clothing, words, music, or mannerisms or even a brand-new giant tattoo (done in an actual tattoo shop, praise be). They are becoming. I never would have believed it would get easier, yet it has—while also somehow continuing to break my heart and inspire me with joy.

What We Can Do

We can appreciate these new versions of our kids that walk through our doors.

I think somewhere inside we all think they are never really going to leave. And then they do. And somehow we survive it. It even becomes normal to us. And when they come home, we might think we are getting them back just as they were. We expect that high school graduate to walk through the door.

My older girls came back as these awesome grown-up versions of themselves—independent versions who sometimes left without thinking to tell us where they were going and when they would return. They liked new music and new people and had new loves. They had rhythms for sleeping, eating, paying bills, and all these adult things. And they were used to doing all sorts of things with their days that we hadn't known about but were now right in our faces. It was time to learn all about the new them.

Like all of us humans doing the good work of human-ing, they are continuing to learn and grow and change. We need to trust that the versions of them who come back to us are built on firm foundations. We have done the heavy lifting, friend. We have put in our time, parented for connection, invested in this relationship, had all the talks, and done all the listening. They know the things. We can now breathe a little and continue to walk alongside them. We can hold their hands and be sounding boards as they learn to be the people God made them to be. You will notice I didn't say the people *we* made them to be. They have always belonged to God, haven't they? We have a front-row seat to the unfolding of His creation, and their coming back is a time to see how they are continuing to become their very own selves.

What Happened for Us

It's all a beautiful walk together with angels singing until humanness enters the scene. When they return and nothing fits together in quite the same way, it can sometimes feel like you have landed a new, not-so-great roommate instead of the kid who left.

My most recent breakdown was all about my two "roommates" who were home all summer. I felt so lucky in my soul to have these kids still coming home. But now they were here, and there was just so much stuff. Bags, bins, and boxes littered their childhood bedrooms and spilled out into the kitchen and the front room and basically all the places. They didn't seem to care about dealing with it. Mostly they were tired, wanting to lie on their beds and read or play on their phones between shifts at work.

I felt like a million people had moved into my house. Adding two kids to the three already there felt strange, and everyone was going in different directions. They all had really good reasons why they didn't have time to scoop the litter box, put away their dishes, or scrub their toilets. I also had really good reasons why I didn't have time to do everything that needed to be done.

I asked and asked and left little notes and set up systems on chalkboards. Nary a thing changed. Then I had a giant freakout with crying and sadness and blaming and all the words in the world. *Why won't anyone just help me?* was the theme of my TED Talk, which was very long and had multiple examples for the audience, who were wholly uninterested in anything other than doing what they could to make my words stop.

My poor secondborn peacemaker's heart could barely take it. I looked at her with guilty eyes because this child had at least attempted some semblance of caring. But once I get going, it is hard to find the off switch. The only way to make it stop in that moment was to excuse myself from the group and let them know I needed to be elsewhere to get my crap together. Todd talked me down. We reminded ourselves that it was just hard, and we walked upstairs, ready to try again.

When I reappeared, my oldest said, "Here's the thing, Mom. It's going to take us a little time to adjust. When I am at my house, I can do my dishes whenever I want and put my stuff away whenever I want. Honestly, I don't really care how clean it is."

Shocker.

She continued, "So we are going to need a little time to adjust, and maybe you can tell us exactly what you want it to be like."

My peacemaker added, "We love you, Mom. We want to be helpful. We just don't always get it or see the same things you do."

Matching their calm and leveled tone, I said, "Think of it like we are roommates. Would you want to live with you? I don't actually care if it is exactly as I want it. I want you guys to be comfy here and not always wondering when I am going to lose it. I just don't want to live with roommates who expect me to do all the things."

They got that it wasn't about us being in charge of them. It was about co-existing in a way that made everyone feel like they could be there and be themselves. We had to have consideration for each other—them for me wanting at least a few clean spaces to breathe, and me for them wanting some places where they didn't have to worry about messes. We are working it out, and this perspective is helping us learn how to respect each other in a new way.

The Good News

The good news when your kids return is that they are back. You get more time. You get to sleep under the same roof even for a few days, and you can make them their favorite foods and tuck them in at night and make them coffee in the morning. It is so fun. Enjoy, learn from them, and maybe listen to some new music, pick up some fashion tips, and listen to their ideas about the world. Talk to them about yours. Then give them big hugs when they are ready to rush out to see their friends. Also, remind them to scoop the litter box if it is their turn.

God goes with them, my friend. And in letting them go, you make your home a place where they want to come back.

Long Story Short

- You will breathe fully again when your kids walk back into your house, and it is a glorious thing.

- They will head out to do their own thing more than you might want them to, but this is normal. They need to be able to live like the adults they are becoming.

- They may come back changed in some ways you didn't anticipate. Find the good in this, and appreciate the new things.

- If the changes bring worry, tread lightly. New adults need to be allowed to stumble a bit, unless there is real danger.

- Think about how you can live with them as roommates instead of as their parents. Bringing your relationship into more equal footing is the next step.

- Love on them where you can, and if all else fails, clean their rooms for them. It will take you one one-hundredth of the time, and they will have a new appreciation for this work you have done for them.

Dear Lord,

Thank You for bringing them back under our roof safely. Please let me remember how I longed for this when I am faced with a million blue bags spilling stuff and when all my glasses go missing and when there are so many people in my house it feels like the kitchen is open both day and night.

Guide us all to find a way to live together, to appreciate and support one another, and to let each of us live in a way that makes our house feel like a respite. Not a dumping ground and not a perfect showcase . . . someplace in between. Help these kids remember to at least let us know where they are going, and let us be able to fall asleep when we're not sure when they will be home.

Please let us appreciate new things about each other, from tattoos on arms to the fact some of us have gotten really into bird-watching. Let these moments be the digging in of the roots that will keep us connected for all the days.

Amen.

CHAPTER 15

When Do They Stop Needing You?

And When Do They Stop Breaking Their Feet?

Honestly, it happens every single time I say it out loud, and this day was no exception. Why do I never learn?

It was a beautiful, sunny Saturday morning, and we were coming off many days of transitioning all the people to all the places and all the things. We were sitting in the aftermath that a busy season brings. Laundry was spilling out of the laundry room. The cupboards were bare. I was trying not to look at my kitchen floor because the sticky stuff on it was from a few weeks ago and I wasn't about to let myself be shamed by vinyl flooring. Bills needed to be paid; the lawn needed to be mowed. We were ready for a productive day to set everything right.

We were also emotionally exhausted. The youngest had started his last year at his beloved elementary school, so every bit of that experience was fraught with emotion. We had been doing the back-to-school things there since Ellie was five, so after seventeen years, we were trying to cherish all the "lasts." Our number four child was starting her first year of high school, which is always huge and comes with navigating new friend things and new classes, routines, and extracurriculars. Our middle kid was beginning his senior year, which we all know is a whole thing. And while all this was happening, we were transitioning our secondborn back to college for year number two in the dorms and our oldest to a new college and into an apartment where she would live with four other women she had never met.

There had been the endless buying, packing, and sorting of things and a lot of driving. So. Much. Driving. This would be our very first weekend with nothing on the calendar, so we were planning to make a nice breakfast before tackling the to-do list.

But it was not to be, and it was my fault. I said it out loud— that thing you never should say: "Toddy, we finally have a beautiful free day! I'm so happy we can eat and relax and get a few things done. It's going to be great!"

Before Todd could even form the words to answer me, my phone rang.

It was the oldest of our people, and it was not good news.

"Hey, Mom, please don't be mad, but I think I broke both my feet."

"Huh?" I swear her words made zero sense to my ears at that moment.

I also noted she asked me not to be mad. This let me know I still had some work to do in our relationship, because I do not want my kids' first reaction to breaking a body part to be worrying that their parents will be mad.

"Honey, when you break bones, I'm never going to be mad.

I love you, and I want to help. But can you say that again? You broke your *feet*? Like plural? Both of them? What happened? Oh my goodness, were you wearing those shoes again?"

Because, you see, she had broken her foot about six months earlier walking around on a big pair of completely dangerous clogs. She had weathered wearing an orthopedic boot during the spring while she was home and somehow managed to still hold down her job at Starbucks. But it hadn't been easy. And now she was not only working but also living in an apartment that was a fifteen-minute walk from campus on a good day. She was only two weeks into classes, and now this.

"Well, actually, yes, I was wearing those shoes. How did you know? I'm so sorry, Mom. I swear I am throwing them away. It was so not worth it."

"Did it just happen? Do you need to go to the doctor?"

"I'll send you a picture of my feet. It happened last night, and I tried just powering through this morning when we went out to breakfast, but I can't even walk on them, Mom. It hurts so bad."

I put her on speakerphone so I could talk to her, let her dad listen in, too, and also look at the pictures of her mangled feet.

They did not look good. I told her to stop walking on them because I was worried she would do more damage. My heart dropped, and I feared the worst.

When Todd walked over and saw the pictures, his eyes filled with tears. "Oh, you poor kid!" he said. "One of us will be right there."

We made a quick plan and got off the phone. Todd and I looked at each other, the makings of an amazing breakfast on the kitchen island between us, my to-do list and pack of pens taunting me from their position next to my computer where only a second ago I had been working and planning all the things this day would bring. "Well, that was my fault for saying we had a free day," I said as I started packing up my purse and looking for a sweatshirt because waiting rooms are always chilly. I knew my day held at least one of these rooms.

I got in the car to pick up my injured twenty-one-year-old baby, while Todd stayed behind to hold down the fort for the rest of the crew, who would get to eat that amazing breakfast. And once again the best-laid plans of parents were thwarted by one of the humans they were parenting.

What We Can't Do

We cannot have the mindset that we will somehow be done parenting. Because it's never-ending. Never. Ending. I was not at all prepared for the marathon of parenting my people. You often hear that you parent your kids for eighteen years, boot them out of the house and into the world where they are suddenly independent, and then travel around to all the places with your significant other and relax and read books. I feel like someone told me this is what would happen, or maybe I saw it on a show. Either way, this was my vision of what parenting would be. I could not have been more wrong.

First, there was nothing magic about a kid turning eighteen. Not one of my kids was more independent or more organized or ready to live on their own when they hit this age. Around here, nineteen also held no magic, and by the time they reached twenty, we had accepted it would be a wait. A long one. Remember that brain research? The brain is not fully developed until a person is twenty-four. And even after that, the needing doesn't end or vanish. I was lamenting to my dad on the phone that it seemed like parenting was getting harder and asking him when they would stop needing us so much. I had to laugh when his answer was, "Well, I can't tell you, dear girl. Because you are in your forties and here you are calling your dad for help."

Well played, Papa, well played. And so true. Not only do my parents still worry about me and come to my assistance, but they also worry about all their grandchildren and help them whenever they can. Perhaps that whole thing about your kids being independent doesn't mean they won't need you. In fact, judging from the amount I talk to my parents, the long haul is going to be a huge reality.

This is just as it should be. God designed families to be interdependent, not independent of one another. We should be one another's people. We should be the ones called when the chips are down, and it is a blessing and an honor to be able to live our own separate lives while also knowing we are always here for one another. I believe God wants us to stay connected to our children even as they become entirely separate from us. This is what He wants in His relationship with us as well. And I think we must find a way to relax and read books in the middle of the madness, because if we try to wait until everything settles down, we will never read or relax again.

If we parent for connection, that connection will see both our kids and us through the hard times. If we know we have created a relationship that is worth them coming back to, we will mourn less when they leave. Our kids will always need us, and at the same time we will always need them. That deep need for connection we have felt from their birth doesn't go away; it just changes form. They don't need us to keep them alive or maybe even pay for everything, and they don't always need us to weigh in on their life decisions. But they need to know we will if they want us to. That they can call us when something awesome happens or when they suspect they have broken both of their feet. They can be more independent and take more risks when they know we are behind them, both cheering them on and being ready to offer support when times are hard.

What We Can Do

We can keep on keeping on. We can't let that magic age of eighteen get stuck in our heads and cause us to think we can't offer our kids what they need because they "should be able to handle their own lives by now." Welp, friend, I should be able to handle my own life by now, yet in the last week I have had to ask for help from my parents, my husband's parents, my husband, friends, and all my children. So, once again, we are made to need one another.

And that two-way street is wonderful and empowering. These kids help me all the time. I need them to pick things up, fix my social media so it isn't "cringy," explain new lingo to me, drive a sibling someplace, make dinner, or get their brother to practice piano. They do so many other things for me—not because I am their mom and I said so (mostly) but because our family strives to live as a team where we all pull the weight for one another whenever needed. The ones who have left are really starting to get this.

I now get to have these beautiful long talks with my second-born that fill up my soul. They are almost always over the phone while one of us is driving. She will talk to me about all that she is learning, figuring out, and thinking about her life or about how her body and soul work best. I couldn't be more here for it if I tried. I adore these calls and hope she will still call me in her seventies, although then I would be in my hundreds.

I watch my most recent eighteen-year-old reaching out for advice as he enters this next phase of his life. He bought his very first car with his hard-earned money, and Todd was there for every step of that decision. Thomas got to decide to buy the car, but good guidance in big decisions is something we all need, and there was no reason for him to wing it just to say he did it all by himself.

I am here to help my kids when they get into a sticky spot with bank accounts or their friends or their classes. And they are here to help their siblings through their trials and to bring me the Headache Hat when they are home and I have a migraine. It is a beautiful and wonderful thing to realize we get to be in this for the longest of hauls.

What Happened for Us

I was talking to Lily right before it happened. I was worrying about her and her dear boyfriend driving in the wintry weather, but I was keeping it light because, as you know, I've learned to be chill and let them live. We chatted about where they were going, and I told them to drive safely and hung up the phone. I told her I was praying over their trip, because that is one of the ways I stay chill—I just hand it over to the Big Guy.

I looked at Todd and said, "I'm getting better, aren't I? I'm okay. She is driving in the snow in a little car, and I am okay. It's like actual progress."

Then the phone rang, and it was Lily again, which was weird. But to my credit my first thought was that maybe she forgot to tell me something. I didn't even worry at first. Even though I should have.

"The first thing you need to know is we are okay," said my wise daughter, who knew that was the best thing to lead with. Then she followed it with, "We just got in an accident, Mom. It was so scary. We went in like a million circles"—maybe not so wise for her to tell me this; I did not need these details living in my brain, but here we were—"and then we landed in a ditch and crashed into a railing. The car is totaled, but we are both okay."

Then came one of the many chill-bump moments I get from God as little gifts: She said, "And, Mom, I could *feel* your prayers keeping us safe. I knew we were going to be okay. I wasn't even scared."

Right?

Even knowing there had been an accident, I was able to hold it together. I wanted to go directly to her. I wanted to throw on my shoes and run out the door, yelling, "Baby, I am *coming!*"

But instead, I looked at my husband, who for once was as rattled as I was. We both took a breath and listened as they called the insurance and her boyfriend's mom, who was closer. I let the people around them care for them and waited to hear that they were safe for the night. I was able to let go and even sleep a little.

Letting go gets easier. They still need you, yes, but the ways they need you change, allowing you to step back and let them go. And the more we practice it, the better we get. Who knew?

The Good News

Our need to be independent and do things on our own is a decidedly Western and American mindset. It is a little dangerous to let this seep into our parenting philosophy, because we don't need to be American parents—we need to be godly ones. God's Word is there to help us build His kingdom here on earth. And that kingdom should look a lot like us loving our kids well and always and them loving us well and always back. That is the dream.

So, even as my people are leaving the nest, we are not living in a way that indicates they are that far gone. Instead, we are always holding space for broken feet and broken hearts, for phone calls from the lonely and from the elated. We are ready at a moment's notice for a kid who just needs to sleep in their childhood bed for a night or who needs us to come and share a meal and look in their eyeballs. We are parenting for the long game, and it is so worth it.

Long Story Short

- You are never done parenting, so settle in. They will still need you, and it is a gift to be asked to help.

- The way they need you may change. Let them lead you to their needs.

- Letting go is hard, but it does get easier with time. I promise.

Dear Lord,

Prepare me for parenting these people who need me in big ways and small ones. Help me to remember to be there by their sides and to let them lead their lives while I fall back into being their support person and forever cheerleader.

Again, I pray You follow them out into the world, guiding their steps and protecting them when they are in cars, when they walk in weird shoes, and when they fall in love and go on job interviews and eventually find people to marry and have kids (when they'll learn what worry really is).

Lord, thank You for the gift of these precious new adults, and thank You for keeping us close. Let me look on in awe as they do all the things, and please keep me from ever saying "I told you so" when they don't listen.

Amen.

A Final Letter

Dear parents of almost growns and growns,

It was bewildering for me to find I was no longer needed for basic things like food and clothing. There were moments of quiet when I didn't know what to do with myself. (The answer is always to *take a nap.*) I feel like one or two big old questions are looming over our heads as we start to launch our people: *How do we return to ourselves and our partners when we are used to giving so much? What will we do with all this love we have that is no longer going to the care and feeding of our people?*

I am going to let you in on a secret that will soothe your soul. Ready? Here it is. . . .

It isn't over.

Not by a long shot. Twenty-two years have passed, and I am still their mom! *Yay!* And you will be too. You will be their parent forever and ever, amen.

How wonderful is that? The clock that has been ticking in our ears, implying that we must enjoy every moment because it will all be over soon, is totally fake. For me, the moment came when the alarm that would signal the end was supposed to go off, and . . . nothing. Not a sound. Every single human that was my child is still my child. There are still moments to enjoy and savor. It will *never* be over. You can settle in and relax and maybe tell your neighbor with littles to relax too. Let's spread this joy.

Our kids still need us. And we still need them. The way we all need each other changes, but it doesn't end. Some of it gets better and better, and some of it gets harder and harder. It is just the way it is. All that love still has a place to go if you stay connected and open to having a relationship with your people that will last a lifetime and serve them in the ways they need you to.

Also, my friends with grandkids tell me that I haven't seen anything yet and that more pure joy is right around the corner. A kind I haven't experienced! What is that all about? I can't wait! (Also, no rush, people.)

As our last pancake enters his teen years, we are older (I feel a lot older, for real) and wiser (*so much wiser*). And while we are savoring his "lasts" in different ways, I am also so much more confident because I know where I am going. I know what I want from all this, and I know what he needs.

Kids need us to show up in their lives for all the days. I am lucky because I have parents and in-laws who continue to show up, and they have really helped us see that this legacy of just being there can go on and on and on. What a gift.

Our families are a gift from God. If we can love one another as He has loved us, starting in our families, the whole world will be a better place.

We will be our kids' jumping-off point and their soft space to land—for all the days if we can.

You will make it (and they will too).

Amy

It's Really Just All About the Love

Early in my marriage, my dear mother-in-law, Lois, often talked of a lullaby she sang to her kids when they were little. When I heard it, my heart cracked a bit with joy and I hoped I'd sing it to my own kids someday. And as soon as my first daughter, Ellie, was born, I sang it to her right there in the hospital room. Tears ran down my face as this moment I had dreamed of finally materialized. My baby wrapped her small, sweet hand around my finger, and I swear she listened to every single word.

The song goes like this:

Mommy and Daddy love sweet little Ellie,
And Grandma and Grandpa—they love you too,

And Momere and Papa and Auntie Nicki—
They all love our sweet little Ellie.

The verses go on, naming all the people who love that new little person: Auntie Danielle, Auntie Molly, Auntie Jessica, and all the Auntie Jennys. A bonus grandma and grandpa. A whole pack of loving uncles. Their cousins. Eventually verses are added for their siblings, pets, teachers, and friends from their playgroup.

As their circle of love grows, so does the song.

We sang it to each of our kids when they entered the world and as they grew older. The longer the song got, the more popular it was, because they knew they were loved . . . and because it could drag a bedtime out. (Score one for them.) But when they got older, the song went silent. No more tucking in, no more singing, no more listing names of love.

From time to time, when things were bad or stressful or hard, I'd ask if they wanted to hear the "I Love You" song. Most often their teenager-ness won out with a sharp "No! I don't want anything right now!"

Don't tell them, but sometimes I would sing it in my head anyway. I'd silently aim it toward them without their permission. A few times, they even gave in. They remembered the feeling the song planted in their hearts. And one actually crawled into my lap, almost crushing my legs and making my heart light as air, and let me sing.

I'd stroke her hair. We'd both remember. And we'd will ourselves back to a simpler time.

One day during one of these moments, my daughter said, "Mom, when things seem really bad and I'm right in the pit, I sing myself the 'I Love You' song over and over and over. I can just feel everyone who loves me gathered around and holding me up. I need that song sometimes to help me."

That love she was able to draw on is exactly what we are trying to give them when we are parenting them into their teenage years.

The whole time they are little, we are just filling them up. But once they're teens, we need to continue filling them with love and memories and experiences. We hope from the bottom of our hearts they'll take all this to their own families one day—even if today they might not seem to be into any of it. The *love* is what we hope and pray and dream they'll carry with them as adults in the world. We desperately want them to know they are wrapped in love and support and are never alone.

Our hard work as parents matters on all the days, in all the moments, and in all the ways. And when our kids are tall and almost grown and are no longer singing lullabies, we see the prints we have left on their hearts—even when the kids are no longer in our homes.

The truth is, all the rules and strategies—or all the things we learned from the ways we were parented—don't really help us unless we do the hard work of knowing everything about these people we are raising. To recognize them as separate humans, not as an extension or reflection of us, we have to know ourselves, too, so we know where we end and they begin. And we need to love them unconditionally, just the way they are, or nothing else will matter. This is how God loves us; what a model we have for this love! He's got us, my friends. I will make it, and you will too.

DISCUSSION QUESTIONS

Chapter 1: The Tricky Tween to Teen Years

1. What was the most unexpected part of your first child entering their tween years? What were you 110 percent prepared for?

2. How did the changes in your child impact you? If you are not quite there, what are some things you might want to think about now, before they get deep into their teens?

Chapter 2: Getting to Know the New Parts of Your Teenager

1. What are some of your favorite parts of the changes in your teenager? How might you let them know you see these?

2. What is challenging about your teenager? How can you deal with these challenges from a place with less emotion? What work do you have to do on yourself?

Chapter 3: Communication and Connection

1. Think of your kids. What is the communication style each prefers? What do you prefer?

2. How can knowing this help you communicate better and stay connected?

Chapter 4: Parenting the First Teenager in Your House

1. Reflect on your first pancake. What would you do differently if you had a time machine?

2. How does learning from your firstborn help you with parenting the rest?

Chapter 5: I Am Not Parenting Myself

1. What were you like as a teenager? How does this impact your parenting?

2. How does the way you were parented impact your own parenting?

Chapter 6: Teens and Friendship

1. Talk about your kids and their friendships. Do they struggle? Do they have positive friendships? What do you pray they find?

2. Do these reflect your own experiences, or are they different? How?

Chapter 7: Cellphones and Social Media

1. What is your current best thinking regarding cellphones and social media?

2. How might you approach this with your people in a way that prioritizes connection and kids owning their decisions?

Chapter 8: House Rules and Chores

1. What house rules do you currently have? How do you want to approach things like chores and curfews with your kids?

2. How can you use connection here to make this a positive learning experience?

Chapter 9: Teenagers and Fashion

1. Is fashion something you bond over or fight over in your house?

2. How do you handle body image in your home currently? What struggles or needs do you have here?

Chapter 10: Teens and Dating

1. What are your expectations around dating?

2. What are the best and hardest parts of your kids' dating lives?

Chapter 11: Teenagers in Church

1. Are your kids questioning their faith? Do you have questions too? How might you approach this together?

2. What are your deepest-held beliefs, and what happens if your kids don't share them?

Chapter 12: When Your Teenager Struggles with Mental Health

1. Let's talk about mental health. Do you have kids that struggle here?

2. How can you support your kids and stay connected to them during these struggles?

Chapter 13: Letting Go

1. What do you want to be intentional about in preparing to launch a kid?

2. What have your feelings been post-launch?

Chapter 14: The First Coming Back, and So It Goes

1. What are you learning about your child now that they have been out in the world?

2. What is your ideal state for your relationship with your child as they go out into the world? (This may be the most important question.)

Chapter 15: When Do They Stop Needing You?

1. How do you see your kids needing you as they grow into full adulthood?

2. What are you most looking forward to or already enjoying about your teens becoming adults?

ACKNOWLEDGMENTS

We are all the sum of the people who have touched our lives, and this leads us to moments like this where I am realizing that I just wrote a whole book and that so many people have supported and cheered me on. It's a moment when a girl realizes she is pretty lucky.

The teacher in me wants to start with you, dear teachers. To all the teachers who have helped me grow and encouraged me as a learner and reader and writer, you have all touched my life and changed me forever. Thank you for doing what you do.

To my colleagues at Kimberly Area School District, you have encouraged me in these same ways, and I am so grateful for your support. And to all the students and their families who have allowed me to be a part of your lives, I thank you from the bottom of my heart.

To my agent, Kristy Cambron, and Rachelle Gardner and everyone at Gardner Literary, thank you for believing in me and for cheering me on. Kristy, thank you for helping me breathe through all the steps leading up to this one. You are amazing, and I wouldn't be here without you.

And to Susan Tjaden, who so thoughtfully and supportively edited her way through too many words, I am so grateful to you and everyone at WaterBrook for taking a chance and guiding my footsteps through all the things for my very first book. I am honored to work with you.

To the team at Her View From Home—in particular, Leslie Means and Carolyn Moore—when you accepted my first piece, I knew I had landed someplace special. You absolutely gave me my start.

To the million wonderful writers whose names would fill a whole page, thank you for the loving support from each of you who has cheered me on, shared my writing, and listened to me as I talked through ideas. You are all the world's best cheerleaders, and I am so lucky to have you in my corner and to be in yours.

To the CSGWNM group—Mikala, Angela, Cassie, Mehr, and Emily—to say this book wouldn't exist without you is the truest thing in the world. The idea for this was born through conversation with you all in Angela's living room. Taking a chance to drive out and meet you in real life was one of my best decisions ever, belly issues and all. I'll never forget how you all hit the ground running to get me out of writing jams, and your feedback helped shape how this book turned out. You all rock.

To my real-life pals—all of you who have sat with me and listened as I have shared about my kids, from the OG playgroup gang all the way to those who have walked beside me and my kids throughout years of theater and sports and have trusted me with your kids as I have trusted you with mine—thank you so much for being a wonderful community.

To Erin Loritz, my teaching and writing partner in crime, thank you for pressing *go* on this whole crazy writing thing on that September day when I sat outside Appleton Rock School when you forced me to be brave. It was a joy writing with you and raising students and then kids together.

To all of you who have read my words and followed my antics online—the Hiding in the Closet with Coffee community and my Hiding in the Closet with Books club pals—you are all a gift. Your comments and stories and just being there have been everything, and I thank God for bringing us all together. You are all that is good about the interwebs.

I want to give a shout-out to my hometown Iron Mountain / Kingsford community: You are all home to me, and the encouragement I have gotten from you has been amazing. Those of you I was a teenager with, thank you for going through the years of big hair and football games and note passing with me. And to all of you who have parented ahead of us and who are cheering us on, thank you for being there for us, leading by example.

To the bonus in-law tribe, Linda, Randy, and all the big bunch of Bunches, you are also a gift, and I wish we lived closer. Our kids love yours, and I cannot even imagine the shenanigans that would ensue.

To my wonderful in-laws, Lois, Denny, Molly, and fam, thank you for your endless support, for getting excited for me, for caring about our kids, for showing me another wonderful way to parent, and for raising an amazing human that I got to marry. I am so lucky to have you.

A deep thank-you to my sisters, Nicole, Jenny, and Danielle: You endured living with me as a teenager (I'm sure just a solid joy) and have endured me talking endlessly about not only this book but also my teenagers. You know the stories behind the stories and are the trusted few for me. I appreciate your wisdom and the way you love my kids, and I'm so lucky to get to watch and learn from you as you parent yours. You guys are a gift. Thanks for marrying great men and having amazing kids who have taught me so much and brought such joy. I love them all.

To my parents, Mary and Tom, there are not enough thank-yous, but mostly right now I am thankful for the way you parented me and for the nonstop support you continue to offer on all the days and in (for real) all the ways. Thank you for loving my kids like you do and for letting them be just who they are. You are a gift and are so loved.

To my kids, thank you for the constant stream of material. The book is now written, so you can just calm it all down. Keep things quiet for a bit, maybe. Nope? Okay, I love you anyway. And man alive, do I also like you. Every one of you is a dream come true, and I thank God above for the exact person each of you is and are becoming. I am a writer without enough words to express my love for you. And you know I really love to say the words. Please feel it in your heart for all the days. You are just everything.

To Todd, the man, the myth, the legend. Who would have thought not only that the girl with the big hair and loud laugh would snag the curly-haired night host but also that we would make five humans from scratch? Go, us! I am so beyond grateful for your endless encouragement, for allowing me to basically ignore everyone for the bulk of the summer, and for carrying the load of dinners and waiting up for kids so I could sleep and have coherent thoughts in the morning. There is no one I would rather do this life with. You make it worthwhile in all the hardest and the best moments—actually, all the moments. I love you, and I like you too. Thank you for tirelessly reading and talking about this book and for being the other half of my heart. Someday it will be quiet around here, and we will have a proper conversation. Until then, it's just been a hard two weeks. We'll make it.

NOTES

1. Lisa Damour, *The Emotional Lives of Teenagers: Raising Connected, Capable, and Compassionate Adolescents* (New York: Ballantine, 2023), 76–78.

2. Cory Turner, "10 Things to Know About How Social Media Affects Teens' Brains," NPR, February 16, 2023, www.npr.org/2023/02/16/1157180971/10-things-to-know-about-how-social-media-affects-teens-brains.

3. Jenny Joseph, "Warning," Scottish Poetry Library, www.scottishpoetrylibrary.org.uk/poem/warning.

4. Daniel A. Cox, "Generation Z and the Future of Faith in America," Survey Center on American Life, March 24, 2022, https://www.americansurveycenter.org/research/generation-z-future-of-faith.

5. 1 Corinthians 13:13.

AMY BETTERS-MIDTVEDT is a *Today Parenting Team* contributing author and speaker with more than a million readers and twenty-five years of experience working with adolescents and families. Both in her job as a literacy coach and in her personal life—where she and husband Todd wrangle their five children—she has been surrounded by kids and teens and is passionate about serving them. She believes strongly that all humans are trying to be their best selves each day, and the core of her beliefs is that the best way through is together.

Amy has a master's degree in leadership, curriculum, and instruction and began her writing journey when she launched her website and social media in 2016. Her work has appeared in many publications online, including *HuffPost*, *Parents* magazine, and *Your Teen* magazine, as well as in the books *So God Made a Mother* by Leslie Means and *In the Trenches: Hilarious Tales of Parenting Gone Awry* by Jen Mearns. You can find her on Facebook, Instagram, and—much to her teenagers' delight—TikTok.